Infidelity

How to Heal From a Traumatic Bond

(How to Forgive a Cheater and How to Help Your Partner)

Ebony McCune

Published By **Jordan Levy**

Ebony McCune

All Rights Reserved

Infidelity: How to Heal From a Traumatic Bond (How to Forgive a Cheater and How to Help Your Partner)

ISBN 978-1-77485-701-4

No part of this guidebook shall be reproduced in any form without permission in writing from the publisher except in the case of brief quotations embodied in critical articles or reviews.

Legal & Disclaimer

The information contained in this ebook is not designed to replace or take the place of any form of medicine or professional medical advice. The information in this ebook has been provided for educational & entertainment purposes only.

The information contained in this book has been compiled from sources deemed reliable, and it is accurate to the best of the Author's knowledge; however, the Author cannot guarantee its accuracy and validity and cannot be held liable for any errors or omissions. Changes are periodically made to this book. You must consult your doctor or get professional medical advice before using any of the suggested remedies, techniques, or information in this book.

Upon using the information contained in this book, you agree to hold harmless the Author from and against any damages, costs, and expenses, including any legal fees potentially resulting from the application of any of the information provided by this guide. This disclaimer applies to any damages or injury caused by the use and application, whether directly or indirectly, of any advice or information presented, whether for breach of contract, tort, negligence, personal injury, criminal intent, or under any other cause of action.

You agree to accept all risks of using the information presented inside this book. You need to consult a professional medical practitioner in order to ensure you are both able and healthy enough to participate in this program.

TABLE OF CONTENTS

Introduction 1

Chapter 1: Definiting Infidelity 4

Chapter 2: Divorce And Separation 17

Chapter 3: Distinctions Between Men And Women (Mental Thoughts, Thoughts, Etc.) 43

Chapter 4: Confession Versus Discovery 54

Chapter 5: Both Sides In The Story 57

Chapter 6: Why Do Human Beings Cheat? 67

Chapter 7: The Reasons To Be Hurt When You Are Being Cheated 84

Chapter 8: Effects Of Betrayal To Our Brain 86

Chapter 9: Feelings Of Jealousy And Anger 89

Chapter 10: From Healer To Destroyer 107

Chapter 11: Learning To Forgive 118

Chapter 12: Rebuilding Trust 126

Chapter 13: Healing Your Marriage 145

Chapter 14: Ideas To Rebuild Sexual Safety 160

Chapter 15: Common Errors To Avoid .. 162

Chapter 16: Resolving The Scores And Giving Up Infidelity 166

Conclusion 183

Introduction

The issue of infidelity and the need to confront it within marriages is now something that's been viewed with stigma and hypocrisy. In the current society and times we live in incidents of infidelity are now more frequent within many marriages. However, only a handful of couples are willing to discuss the issue, and even fewer to face it honestly and openly the issue. Within the dynamic of every romantic relationship the risk of infidelity is an actual issue that couples must face and confront.

Infidelity is a fact that has raised the ugly side of infidelity in numerous structures and social situations. It has crossed the lines of race, class gender, or religion. It has stepped into the homes of families, churches as well as the white house the political campaigns and even groups, and the results in many marriages are undisputed.

One of life's biggest problems is recovering from a shady relationship. There is a gap in your own self and don't know what to do to alleviate your grief. There is no way to know what causes a relationship to go sour or why certain people stay with one another and others do not. To be loved and loved is an amazing feeling, but once you discover that everything you had thought about or planned is illusionary, your whole life is destroyed. The feeling of being betrayed is like a cold blade cutting into your soul. However, regardless of your suffering, pain and rage there is always the chance of rebirth. The process of healing from infidelity can require a lengthy period of time, possibly months or even years, but when you are willing to work hard to it, you'll be able recover and enjoy a fulfilling life.

If you've been fortunate enough to go through this emotional turmoil and loss, this book is designed to alleviate your grief. There isn't a universal solution for helping people recover from their infidelity, but there are certain methods by that you'll be able to manage your life once more.

If someone realizes that they've been duped in an affair, it takes some time to come to the truth and view life from a different viewpoint. Once you've come to acceptance of the reality and you've cried as hard as you are able to and you've had enough, the first thing you can do is to get back to yourself. You must remind yourself that there is much more than a broken relationship. There is no way to convince yourself that you're better than the status quo you been settling for. It is your responsibility to build the courage to face the truth and set off on a path of self-discovery. So, take off your socks and start the next chapter of your life.

Chapter 1: Definiting Infidelity

To define "infidelity" by one definition is complicated because the circumstances of infidelity differ from person to. In most cases, infidelity can be described by the term "cheating" as well as "having the desire" with another. It is believed that one is engaged in infidelity if they are not totally loyal to their partner, however there are many other ways to define"infidelity"

Sexual attraction is among the most frequent indications of infidelity. Sometimes, people develop an attraction to an individual even though they is a committed partner whether they're married or dating. Infidelity happens when someone experiences a sexual attraction to someone else and is able to act on it rather than trying to get rid of these negative feelings.

An emotional connection that is romantic It is believed to be cheating when he/she creates a romantic connection to someone different from their current partner. The connection may manifest through a variety of methods, including through gestures or a believing that the person is the one he/she would like to spend time with.

Untruthfulness - Despite the sexual attraction or the emotional connection between another person, there are people who claim that their partner is committing infidelity if they believe that he/she is dishonest with them. For instance, they may do not know important information when they talk to their spouse, yet they disclose these missing details to a different person. Another instance could be that they're having a conversation with someone in private or having dates and not communicating with their partner about it. The act of lying to a partner can indicate that something isn't right in their relationship. Distrust is an indication of a weakening relationship, especially when you would rather share your experiences with others rather as opposed to your partner.

The question of cheating is based on the viewpoint of the spouse. If someone is hypersensitive and apathetic, even the only the tiniest connection to someone or someone else could signal infidelity. Infidelity, however, is a major mistake, and can cost your relationship and can cause a lot of hurt and anxiety for you as well as your partner. Furthermore, infidelity can cause your partner to lose trust for the rest of your life. If you're lucky then you'll be able to get this trust. If you're not lucky, then you've lost your relationship for good. Because of this, the goal in this guide is to give suggestions on how you can combat infidelity, restore your trust in your partner and salvage your deteriorating relationship.

Infidelity is the root of many causes.

If someone discovers that their partner is cheating on them or her partner, they might ask these questions: "Why? Do I have something to do with it?" "Am I not sufficient?" "What did I have done to deserve this?" There is no comprehensive list of the answers to these questions, as and the reasons for infidelity. However, here are the most frequently asked questions that are separated into emotional and physical aspects that can help you to answer your concerns:

Emotional component

* Incompatibility is one of the most common reasons individuals cheat is because they're not getting along with their current partner , however they don't want to end their relationship because they believe they'll "work issues out". But, in some cases, things don't get it right and the person finds themselves looking for someone else to meet his needs for emotional fulfillment, but not realizing that they are committed to a different person.

* Emotional connection that is romantic - If a person has a romantic relationship with another person and they are able to get along there is a chance that they will establish a strong romantic emotional bond without even having to ask. As they begin to get to get to know one another it is possible that someone will feel someone else is who is fun to spend time with and could be a great partner in lieu of the person he/she is currently in a relationship with.

* Boredom and weariness A common reason for people cheat is because they're tired of their

relationship because they're already bored. When someone feels that there's nothing new happening they could leave and search for someone who can bring them back that "excitement".

Physical aspect

"Sexual attraction" In relation to the physical aspects that is infidelity the main causes of infidelity and break-ups in relationships is the desire to sexually attract toward someone other than the partner currently in love. Everyone has their desires and fantasies, but occasionally individuals are unable to stifle these desires, even when they are aware that they're still in love and that's why they will cheat on their spouses as they attempt to fulfill their desires.

* Time spent shared - Partners may not have the exact career paths. They interact with different people each day and spend the majority of their time with different kinds of people. But, if someone spends time with a person it is possible that they'll form a bond with one another and especially in the event that their interests match

well and they don't let themselves be restricted by prior commitments.

* Absence - Having to spend a lot of time away from your partner may create a sense of longing and the majority of the time this "longing" is the root of infidelity, as it is common to search for someone to fill the "gaps" in their relationship that the partner has left behind.

* Long-distance relationships - It's difficult for relationships with long distances to thrive, particularly in the event that one person isn't up-to-date on the actions and activities of their counterparts. Like absence, relationships that are long distance can only endure because one of the two looking at romance and excitement without thinking about their partners. Sometimes it is due to the belief that they'll never be caught due to the distance between both of them.

These are only a few reasons for infidelity. There are many more. However, the thing that must be remembered is that whether caught or not whether secret or not the act of cheating is still cheating. cheating is a serious crime to commit against one's spouse, and there can't be any legitimate reason for cheating, because if two people could trust and respect one another, there is no reason to seek out another person to perform the task.

What should you do when you realize that your partner has been caught in an affair

The most obvious reaction one can experience when they find the cheating partner is anger and shock. It is normal for a major fight to ensue and there will be many tears or blaming and explanation. But, yelling at each other and not letting one explain, or simply crying is not the best solution to deal with infidelity. What is the best way to react when they find their spouse being infidelity?

Keep calm

This advice might seem like a joke to some and yet it's an extremely crucial aspects to remember when you are dealing with a shaky partner. It is crucial since you will be able to be able to think clearly if you've got an unhurried mind. It will keep you and your partner from embarrassment if you cause an incident if you're in a position to maintain your calm regardless of the severity of the incident.

Engage your partner

The act of confronting your partner doesn't mean going into their room throwing things around and shouting at him/her to ask them who the other is. Engaging with your partner is about seeking out honest responses from them. The confrontation must be conducted with precision, especially important if you are on your own. If you confront your partner by beating, shouting, or other violent methods is likely to create a fight and prevent both of you from discussing issues. That's the reason it is essential for you to approach your partner with calmness.

Don't allow anger to cloud your judgement.

It's natural to feel angry if you find your partner doing something wrong, and who wouldn't? If you truly are determined to correct the situation it is essential to take the time to listen and attempt to understand the words your partner may say. allowing your anger to obscure your judgment and prevent you from fully understanding the words spoken by your partner will not help you as being a narrow-minded person will not help your relationship.

Let your partner provide you with the information.

The most important thing you'd want to find out when you spot someone cheating on you is of the cheating. Be aware that you'll never know the reason if you don't allow your partner to explain the situation why they did it in the first place. Although it's an error to make you, your partner still is entitled to an explanation. The advantage of hearing others' explanations is that you'll be able to evaluate your decision more carefully based on the explanations of their partner and also learn important life lessons throughout the process. Perhaps, for instance, your spouse has cheated on you due to the fact that there's something wrong with your behavior and he's not happy with and would rather search at an alternative. Hearing this type of explanation might be painful but at the end, it will show you what went wrong , and it will help you understand the steps you need to take to rectify the situation.

How to deal with infidelity

When you, along with your spouse reach a consensus in spite of the affair one of you was involved in you would like to save your marriage. It is important to acknowledge that your relationship before the affair was one that is worth keeping and you feel it's worthwhile to fight for it. After you have reached the decision, there's a few issues you'll have to take into consideration and follow through with.

1. The first thing to be completed (obviously) is to bring the relationship to an be ended. It's not possible for a relationship that is working in the event that there is a third party involved. There shouldn't be any casual meeting with that person in the event of the possibility of a slip-up. If the person was a office coworker, it might be wise to consider changing the position.

2. It will not be an easy job to get the pieces back together and put it back together again. Therefore, be aware that there may be tension,

and some fluctuations and ups. It is important to navigate through it calmly and not be scared at the very first crash that happens.

3. If you're the one who been involved in an affair and you want to talk about it and you want to discuss it, discuss it in a candid and honest way. A lack of evasive responses or half-truths will aid in this situation. In fact, it could be extremely detrimental to your relationship right now If you're not fully truthful.

4. Also, you must hold your spouse accountable right now. It is common that your spouse will suffer from concerns about trust. If your partner is in need of constant assurance and must be aware of your location constantly, then you must provide the necessary information. The expectation that trust will be restored instantly is not a sensible idea.

5. You must swear in a sincere way that this will never be repeated. If your partner has to hear this a few times, it should be explained and discussed.

6. The way forward must be determined by the person who has been who has been trampled. If

the person who was betrayed (the person who has been sacked) requires some time, it should be granted and the one who is the one who had the affair must be more sensitive and understanding.

7. The party who was the victim of the affair must reflect about the reason for the incident. What was the reason for him/her to wander? It could be something that must be altered so that it is not to occur again.

8. In order to move forward, it is the duty for both parties. The responsibility cannot rest on one person. Both partners must work hard and focus on their marriage to ensure it is a success.

9. Consider going to couples counseling or therapy for marriage. A good therapist you trust can be a blessing for you. It could be beneficial to discuss your concerns with an impartial outsider in making decisions instead of having emotional, heated discussions with yourself.

10. Be compassionate with yourself and with your partner. Spend time with each other, nurturing in your relationships.

After you have made the choice to stay together, put in on it. You've both agreed that it will be difficult , but you have determined that what you have merited fighting for. Don't be discouraged by the initial difficulties and don't allow anyone to tell you that it cannot be accomplished. It is possible, and you must believe in it, in order to succeed.

Chapter 2: Divorce And Separation

Definition of divorce and separation

Separation is simply an instance where couples who are married live apart in accordance with an order of the court that permits the couple to remain legally married.

Divorce is the end of a legally binding marriage with a court ruling and the court will require both parties who seek divorce to provide legal and valid reasons.

Divorce causes

Infidelity

One of the main reasons for divorce is extramarital relationships. These could cause a marriage to fall apart faster than reasons other than. There are various reasons for cheating, even though the reasons for cheating could be easily overlooked.

In some cases, spouses might resort to cheating out of anger or resentment, or it could be a retribution for a previous offense. Whatever the reason cheating against your spouse is inexcusable. divorces continue to occur all over the globe due to spousal infidelity. A lot of people find it difficult to forgiving. It's difficult, to let go and forget the hurt caused by an unfaithful partner. It's even more difficult to view the situation from their point of view.

Money

People's views can shift around the subject of money. The issue regarding money, and deficiency of it could cause many nagging issues to surface in marriage. Money can stress the marriage in a variety of ways, ranging from the spending habits of spouses to conflicts with regard to financial goals or a the power struggle that arises from the one who makes more money and the issues could get worse. The issue of money can create lots of pressure on a relationship. If the debts pile up and the spouses do not understand the other's position on the one who has put in more effort to pay them off and a problem develops. The issue can reach its most extreme and can be unbearable to final.

Insufficient communication

I'm not sure if that marriage can exist without communication. It is the foundation on the which it is built. Insufficient communication could result in resentment, and to anger and frustration between spouses. This could negatively impact the entirety of a marriage. If communication in the marriage is strong, however it is the base for creating an ongoing relationship. Inability to communicate effectively is also a concern. If spouses are in a bad way, like shouting at each other, or nagging, or engaging in tiny conversations, they are setting the way for more issues in their marriage. A proactive approach to halting stagnant communication in any relationship is to practice mindfulness. Engaging in mindful communication and jotting down behaviors that are not working for you and your partner is essential in bringing your marriage back to be successful. It's not an easy task to accomplish, but it's worthwhile to strengthen and keep your relationship intact. If you wish for your marriage to be successful it is essential to speak with your spouse. It is essential to sit down together and discuss issues, regardless of how difficult they may seem. Making decisions and resolving problems by yourself can make your spouse feel as though you've edged the other out. The silence of a spouse can lead to bigger issues in a relationship. This is why it's crucial to show appreciation when your spouse pays the respect they deserve during your marriage or whenever they engage with you.

Constant disagreements

Incessant argumentation can lead to the end in your marriage. We fight over a variety different things, some are as basic as who gets to do what chores and the best school to admit our children.

The majority of times, arguments could be the result of an internal feeling that you are not heard. If we're unable to look at things from the other person's viewpoint and this causes constant arguments and the constant fighting can destroy relationships.

The absence of a courtship

It's a good eyebrow-raising idea to discuss, however it could take an otherwise happy marriage down. Courtship is the time that couples begin to get acquainted with one another. As we grow older we feel the butterflies greater and we're full of love and affection. This is why we don't take the time to meet each other before deciding that we have to be in love. We hurry to be married. It's not that it's the norm for everyone, however for those are rushing to get married makes us aware of the flaws of our partners that we are unable to address too late during the process. Without the time of courtship and dating they are not becoming acquainted with the personality lifestyle, habits, and perspectives of one another. Courtship provides the opportunity for young lovers to understand their motives towards each other. Are they really in love with their partner? This is also the perfect opportunity to get to know what they are like. The ability to live together is the main reason for a happy marriage, or any other relationship. The reasons that couples get married differ, but they each one of them denies them the opportunity to truly get to know the person they are marrying and whether or not they would be able to live together. These reasons, along with the pressure from society to marry are not helping to keep the couple in a relationship.

Unrealistic expectations

Unrealistic expectations can makes relationships difficult. While it's not difficult to make an extensive list of things you would like your spouse to be and do once you get married, they are likely not capable of being this. What happens when they are not able to be met are that they stress both of you and lead to unnecessary conflicts to start to develop. This could make both of you vulnerable to fail. They're likely to fall short of your expectations of them.

Unprepared for the wedding

Couples of different ages have complained about the lack of preparation as the reason for why their marriage ended with divorce. Couples who are in their twenties suffer the highest divorce rate , and the majority of divorces happen within the first 10 years of marriage. They occur more frequently between 8th and 4th year of wedding.

The reality of entering into marriage without proper preparation is not unique to any particular group of people or regions across the globe. People who are young make the mistake of thinking that they are comparing the preparations for marriage with their physical development. This is why they get married on the spur of the moment instead of preparing for the life-changing decision. The lack of preparation, whether it's emotionally, psychologically or even intellectually is one of the main reasons marriages do not work. The lack of understanding the commitments, obligations, care and the communication that relationships require and more specifically, what their relationship needs creates an unbalanced relationship that leads to divorce nearly inevitable.

Intimacy is lacking

The marriage will lack intimacy when either or both of the partners are not able to feel connected to one another. When you eliminate intimacy, being married may be like living with a stranger or with roommates. It could be emotional or physical, and a partner who keeps ignoring one another and refusing to communicate with them could result in bigger problems. The more you bond, the better. This is a task that is shared by both partners. Both of you must be willing to make special memories within your relationship. Learn to speak each other's language of love and make a commitment to each other that show kindness and cause your spouse to view your love for each other. Intimacy problems can quickly end a marriage. It is important to meet with your partner and talk about the specific ways you will overcome your issues with intimacy. Discuss with your partner what your sexual fantasies are, and then seek out ways to manage your sexual desires with each other. Be aware that intimacy isn't just about sex.

Lack of responsibility/one-sided responsibility

An individual's refusal to take on accountability or one having more responsibility than the other could cause problems in the marriage. This can cause one person resent one. Each couple has their own tasks to handle and distinct strategies for handling them, however having a conversation with your spouse to discuss these and come to an agreement on who will manage what is a good way to maintain your relationship in the right perspective.

Abuse

Some couples' reason for them to divorce and is believed to be a valid and solid reason is that the relationship is violent. When one spouse is emotionally or physically or emotionally abusive, the other may be looking to end the relationship. There's no reason they should not. The spouse who is being abused must seek assistance as quickly as they are able to.

Whatever the cause of the abuse, don't accept it. It is crucial to exit the abusive situation as quickly as possible. The abusive partner can quickly get out of control, and the best option is to get out.

Physical , and often emotional or verbal abuse is among the reasons that make many marriages end in failure. This requires very sophisticated methods to deal with the problem.

The advantages of divorce

Divorce can be so difficult that we may be incapable of seeing any possibility to be found. It is, after all, an unhappily clouded and tense situation, one that can be emotionally and life-altering. We're more focused to dismiss it as that is not necessarily evil.

If we view divorce this way, we take longer to realize the potential in the process. We are less likely to realize that something good could happen to us because of it. This is the reason I've taken the decision to discuss what benefits divorce can bring and what positive outcomes we should be looking for in the divorce circumstance. What are the advantages of divorce? Here are a few that I've discovered.

Self-time is more important.

The divorce process gives you more time to focus on your own needs. After divorce your time spend with your spouse and your family your goals will quickly come back to you and you are able to utilize it to pursue what you love to do. While at the same time you'll have more time to reflect and self-evaluation.

Freedom

When you're married it's easy to appear irresponsible. But this isn't the case if you're recently divorced. There is a lot of freedom in your lifestyle to do everything you want to explore, without limitations.

Earn extra cash

Okay, I wasn't saying this in any way. If you're going through divorced, you are able to discuss property and child support, as and maintenance to ensure that you'll be looked after until the divorce. This will help to lessen the shock of becoming a single person once more.

You might just fall in the love of your life again

Divorce may reveal to you the areas you have to improve at and provide you with the opportunity to improve these areas which means that within no time you will be back and in a more positive and more promising relationship. Make sure to not jump into this.

The disadvantages of divorce

The stigma of divorce is that it's being a disaster, but is it that divorce mean to us that we desperately need to leave. There are a few of them:

The loneliness

Divorce is when you and your happily married partner are now going their separate ways. It is no longer possible to do things together and the hopes you shared are immediately gone. Now, you'll be doing many things on your own and it can quickly turn into a extremely lonely. If divorce is new the situation can seem difficult to navigate.

Children

The psychological and emotional trauma children experience during divorce is enormous and they sometimes traverse the entire process by themselves. In certain communities they can become a target for ridicule and may be apprehensive about being different from everyone who are around them. They also experience a lack of loyalties and are unsure of how to manage that. If it is not handled properly divorce could be a long-lasting impact on children as well as their outlook on love and life throughout their adult lives.

Health degeneration

If your divorce is a disaster it is important to pay extra attention to looking at your health. The divorce process can lead to depression and thoughts of suicide. It is important to ensure that you're emotionally stable to ensure that you don't have problems with your health in the future.

You must change your circle of friends

The divorce process forces you to reorganize your life. As you try to make a change you'll need to make changes to your friends as well as the people whom you hang out with. You'll need to stay away from those friends the couple had in common and then make new friends. Divorce means you must begin to build a your own social circle that has no relationship to your spouse.

Contributions to the financial divorce process

Divorce is a significant expense. It can drain your finances. Employing an attorney or arbitrator can cost you some money. Following your divorce, you may wish to start thinking about rebuilding your finances once more.

The healing process from the pain of divorce

Accept Reality

Your partner isn't coming back. It's difficult and hurts to admit it, but sat there waiting and praying for them to return is likely keep you suffering. There have been instances where couples were divorced and the spouse who started the divorce process realized that they committed a mistake and they could not live without their spouse. Then they returned begging. It's the perfect ending that we'd all like to see However, the research on marriage remarriage after divorce indicates that it is only happening in 1percent of instances. So why do you want to wait for something that is only the chance of occurring? The most beneficial thing you can do is acknowledge that your partner has left and will not be returning. The sooner you're in a position to accept with the reality of this the simpler it will be to proceed to the next chapter in your lives.

Be aware that you are grieving.

The emotions you feel after divorce are similar to the feelings you'll experience following the loss of a beloved one. You can ask anyone who has gone through both of these experiences and they'll inform you that it's almost exactly the same. Another thing for you to take note of by this experience is the majority of people who experience grieving stages always make it through it. At first there are days when you'll feel helpless and the end result will appear to be grim. There are certain to be more positive days to come. Even if you can't see it right now, you can be sure that peace and relief will gradually be restored in your home. Grief is not something that happens in a linear fashion. It's totally normal to have good and bad days. We all do! Making a step forward but then having to step back can be okay so long as you continue moving forward on your path towards recovery.

One step at an time.

At this point in your life, it's likely overwhelm you emotionally and mentally. you to consider what this could be like in five, ten and twenty years. It's not necessary to know everything in the span of a single day. Relax, let go and take it each day as it comes. It will be time to consider the big picture when you're prepared. At first, stay with the tasks you can manage. Every time you face an overwhelming long-term concern that causes you to feel overwhelmed try to gently keep in mind "One day at an time" and take several deep breaths to focus your attention on the moment in which you are.

You can forgive your partner

There is no right not to be bitter, angry or sad. The divorce process is often a betrayal of your trust as well as an unfulfilled promise, therefore you're entitled to be upset, but if you hold on to the pain and anger, you're harming yourself, more importantly, the person you are hurting. It is best to accept your partner's apology. It's not easy, but you need to think that they have done what's best for them. You have to take the best decision for yourself too by letting go and forgiving. Many people are under this misconception that if you let someone else forgive you and accept their forgiveness, it implies that they're free from the responsibility. They believe this can be a way to let them off the burden.

In reality, it's contrary. If you are willing to forgive, regardless of whether your partner is aware or not, you're giving yourself the chance to live a new life. This is your method of breaking the chains that are shackling you to this broken relationship as well as your partner.

Stop all contact

The person you are talking to is trying to make a change in their life, but you're snooping around, checking their social media accounts to find out what's happening with them and also who they've left you for. You're throwing up tantrums as you try to cause their lives difficult. It's a negative way of coping that could affect you far greater than your spouse. It's not helpful to your emotional well-being to keep doing the same thing. Don't allow another person to have the power to influence you. Your self-esteem and dignity are crucial therefore you should quit talking to them, sending them letters and attempting to make acquaintances with them. You are able to be friends, of course, but that will be after you've healed emotionally. Right today, your only one you'll need is you and your true friends, not your ex-partner who has chosen to leave your relationship.

Create a relationship with you

It's true that if you don't feel like you love yourself, appreciate yourself, or believe you're worth spending time with no one will want to share these experiences with you. Are you able to imagine wanting to be with someone who's always unhappy, angry or downright miserable? It's possible that you'll be fine with that for a brief time, but then it just feels like a drain on you.

What you really need now is not a re-engagement or making others pay for the things your ex did. What you require today is to be able to love yourself, care for yourself , and be kind to yourself. It is important to learn to be independent and accomplish things independently. I'm not saying that it's going to be simple or effortless- at the beginning, it can be a bit difficult, particularly in the case of not having been single before or had an ex-partner for a while however, it's not that difficult at the beginning. After a few months you'll start to appreciate it and want to spend time alone. If you're looking to start a new relationship, it can aid in evaluating your prospective partner more thoroughly, so you'll be able to make informed choices , and not simply jump into a relationship due to feeling not happy or in need of a partner.

Get help from a professional if you need to be.

In certain circumstances there may be a need to consult an experienced marriage counselor, especially in the case of some sort of abusive marriage or through a particularly painful event. After divorce, the most effective option is to turn your attention back to your self and begin to love yourself once more. Loving yourself is taking good care of your self and becoming the very best version of you. If you need help to achieve this, it's acceptable to talk to an expert. Don't be entangled in the stigma of it and risk your health and wellbeing.

A professional will be able to assist you through the hurt of these experiences, to allow people to accept the loss and forgive your ex and get forward with your life.

Watch out for kids

One of your biggest worries in the aftermath of divorce is the children. It is your fear that they will not be able to deal with the divorce in a healthy way and could start acting out or getting into trouble. If you allow yourself to be a victim of emotional trauma and allow them to witness yourself in a state of distress you will be emotionalally wounded, but if you take care to handle the divorce in a positive manner and protect your children from the hurts and trauma, and remind them the fact that both you and your ex-partner chose to do it for the best reasons option, they'll be able to deal with the divorce as well. Be a role model for your children throughout the divorce process and talk with your partner how to keep their mental and emotional well-being a top priority, so that your children can get over divorce swiftly and grow into more successful versions of themselves. To ensure that your children succeed after divorce, it is important to stay healthy since you are their backbone as well as their role model. If you fall and they break, they will too. However, research data have shown that the majority of children can cope well when they go through a divorce. What your children will do and react to divorce is entirely up to you and your spouse.

Your emotions are safe

However we wish to look at divorce, it is merely a means of ending an affair that has turned to the side of bitterness. In the end, whether you're who initiates the process or receiving it , if you are both going through a divorce, it's crucial to be aware of your emotional ride. Make sure you're not doing something that you regret or damage the emotional position of your ex-partner.

If you've gone through divorce and had the divorce regardless of how it ended it was, you'll want to be aware of your feelings. You'll need to manage your negative emotions so that they don't harm your self-esteem completely. Being in control of these negative thoughts is primary goal of helping you to achieve complete recovery. The emotions in this category will be quite high however, you should reduce your negative emotions to the extent you can to ensure they're not harming your. To do this, you'll need be aware of the triggers that trigger your emotions; specifically those that trigger negative emotions. What causes you to feel these emotions continuously when it appears like you be healed? What are you looking for? What should you avoid doing? Here are a few suggestions to aid you in separating these issues and help protect your feelings so you don't feel affected by divorce or your ongoing relationships with your former spouse following the divorce.

Do not refuse to communicate with your ex

The desire to hate your spouse will be very increased after divorce. Do not give into this since hate is an unwholesome emotion that can cause self-harm. Showing your partner that you hate them can also have the effect to cause this feeling to be passed on to your children. I don't think you'd like this. No one wants to do that. So , please, don't dislike your spouse. One way you could show your hatred for your spouse is to not observe them. It could be seen as undeveloped if you have children between you. If it's not an abusive relationship, and you share children You should be able to balance feelings of pain and be able to communicate with your spouse whenever you need to. If your spouse calls you, you should respond with manners. Once there was the love of your life.

Stop looking around for who to be accountable

Your relationship is way beyond the point where you need to look at who is responsible for the issue. The most important thing to think about now is how you can move forward in your journey. Find out who's at fault could only bring back your hurts and make you be hurt even more.

Let it be. Perhaps , what you must be aware of is that you're certainly not the sole one suffering. Your ex-partner is suffering as well , and it isn't easy to make the choice of leaving your spouse.

Be aware of your actions before you make them.

Today, more than ever, it is important to take the time to take well planned choices. Do not let your emotions rule your life as they can lead you to make decisions which you later regret.

Do not believe or believe that you are a saint through the entire process

The idea that everything was the fault of your ex-partner's fault hinders your growth through the process. Be open to seeing the actions you took which led to the breakup of your marriage . Then, try to figure out the way that you can alter your behavior to improve your life to avoid repeating the same mistake.

Do not truncate any attempts to reconcile

In the event that your spouse trying to fix the situation, don't be the reason why your efforts aren't working. Reconciliation is possible,, but be aware of your own best interests. Ensure that any compromise you make will benefit both of you.

If you decide to end the divorce, be sure to be consciously forgiving your spouse for the harm they caused you through the marriage as well as the divorce. You should be willing to forgive since it is only at this point that you are able to truly let go. Resentment is only going to hinder your progress. behind.

Maintain your expectations in check

Expectations are the reason behind the majority of difficulties in relationships. If you're expecting something your spouse will not provide, you're bound to get into problems. That's why you need to be aware of your expectations. Expectations can go off the rails during the divorce process and after. Be aware that no one knows the expectations you have until you let them know and your spouse cannot be legally bound to fulfill your expectations. Instead of accumulating expectations on your chest be open to change and one that is able to adapt to the circumstances at any time even if you're not getting exactly what you're looking for or expecting.

Chapter 3: Distinctions Between Men And Women (Mental Thoughts, Thoughts, Etc.)

How can we solve the issue When an individual woman is confronted with a problem, she'll tell her partner, friend or husband, or someone at the front of the bus. Some people write their thoughts in the journal, write a note to someone else, or create an update on a social networks. Women believe that when the issue is discussed, it is easy to fix or "steal your heart". What can an individual do if he encounters trouble? The answer is that he'll not do anything, he'll lay on the sofa and watch the television and be silent. Men will distract themselves from their problems and once they are calmer they'll begin to exercise and, naturally, on their own. For gentlemen, this suggestion makes them feel overwhelmed.

If men are upset or depressed, they keep their silence. The silence of men always causes women to be afraid. However, when women are upset or sad, they'll be crying and everyone should know that tears are a dangerous weapon.

Emotional Ability: It's believed that women can discern the expressions, images and signals of the people who are around them quickly. If a woman enters the room with a lot of people she will be attentive to and be able to recognize facial expressions, moods and the attitudes of everyone. The men, on the other hand, are intent on spotting familiar faces that they love or don't like.

Basic Brain Distinction: If men tend to think of technical matters, sports, and particularly sexuality, women are more focused on sharing and fashion.

An improved comprehension of space: In males their brains are better in recognizing space and concentration as well as sense of. This means that the coordination of eye movements, hand movements rotation, and stability are superior as compared to women. In contrast male brains are also able to handle abstract information for example, reading instructions and maps better than women's brains.

Perception: Men's brain is a logical, analytical mind. They believe that the work ethic is greater than any words. Women are intuitive and genuine. The word is crucial.

The women "hear" greater than the men. Johns Hopkins University study found that males tend to be 5.5 percent more likely suffer from hearing loss than women, whereas hearing abilities for infants for both genders isn't much different. Men lose hearing of high-frequency sounds, while women lose their hearing capacity in low frequency. Researchers believe these changes result from the influence of environmental factors and lifestyles.

The prevalence of autism in women is significantly lower than that of men. In reality experts claim that autism is more prevalent among males than females. However, experts are unable to provide an exact answer. There are two different ways of thinking: The first is that the idea is that women suffer from only some mild forms of autism. Therefore, women are able to hide their "problems" while men suffer from autism all the time A second belief is that the modern lifestyle that has more rigid social standards can make men stressed out and more susceptible to developing autism.

Recalling information: Women's memory is like a huge chest of drawers, and everything is organized. Women remember precisely the information they have about the majority of people they've met as well as all the events that have occurred. For instance the date of birth of a loved one acquaintances, what kind of food they'd like to consume or what their children require at the classroom. Don't forget to give these things to women and they'll take care of it. In short it is true that women's memory is excellent. Contrastingly, men tend to only recall what they perceive as significant.

Do several different things simultaneously Men typically concentrate on one thing for instance, if he's shaving and you wish to inquire about, then there won't be a response. However, women are able to do a variety of things simultaneously. There are some who suggest that the brain functions of the genders of men and women is different because their roles in the family in the past was distinct. Men have played an important part in the family's life thousands of years ago, and they could not be focused solely on hunting. However, women were different. They needed to take care of their children, educate them on what they were, aid others, and so on. Even to today, despite the fact that society has evolved so dramatically and developed, this tradition is still alive. It is said that "women have three heads and six hands".

Sensitivity to sounds: In a test carried out to assess the hearing abilities of men and women experts were unable to determine that women or men have a higher "sensitive" to sounds. Women can hear babies cry , while men lay back in bed like nothing has happened. If, for instance, you heard a cat crying on the street there is a chance that women's hearing was higher than of males. However, since "heroes" have the capability to direct the sound well. They will also be able to demonstrate to women that the cat is moving in which direction.

Normal men are aggressive and strong , however, standing before women is stiff, stuttering and stammering. Normal women are shy but when they meet males, and they become the top-performing.

Men like to take on innovative work, and the wind, but stop, take a breath and relax and relax in between. Women like boring, repetitive, and more consistent work as opposed to males.

For males, they fall in love with ease when they first met, and it is evident on their faces, but women, it is common to go back and forth with men repeatedly to fall in love.

Men in their early years are drawn to having a wide range of acquaintances, however women are able to connect with more of their friends in the middle stage of their lives.

If you're involved in been involved in an affair, ladies will spend money on beauty products and shopping. If they're cheated on, they declare divorce. Men however make use of funds in order to "care" to their spouses. If they're beaten, they'll reconsider as they don't wish to destroy the house.

While shopping, men decide to purchase new shoes, and they will buy a pair. The ladies initially wanted to purchase a dress, however later, they end up buying an array of clothes.

At 7 pm, women will take a bath and put on makeup for about 2 and a half hours, but they are still not finished. Men might take about 10 minutes for their preparation and will be dressed before women.

At the moment of entering the restaurant Men go to the bathroom only to attend to their requirements as well as wash their hands. The women in the toilet perform a variety of things like combing their hair, applying makeup and calling, chatting and texting.

If they argue, men quickly heal in five minutes, but If women were once in a fight for 10 years, 10 years later, you will see the scorn on her face.

Men are able to poke around but their bond is always permanent. Face-to-face women are always friendly and behave in a manner that is friendly, however their relationships is not going to last forever.

When assessing a man's character women typically consider several things: humor, intelligence and financial capacity as well as the shape. Contrarily, men judge women based on appearance. look at the importance of appearance. This can be an obstacle to her intelligence or her humor.

Color perception: An intriguing study shows that women are able to recognize and differentiate a vast array of colors, whereas men could only distinguish a handful of basic colors.

Men pick faces, women select hearts. This is because of the face, males don't want to negotiate for sales due to the appearance, they can get money to treat clients or lie to clients. For women, they appreciate the genuine heart of the gentlemen and not the pomp on the outwardly.

Men prefer quantity, women prefer quality: Women appreciate the quality of their marriage instead of the monthly sum you earn than or less. Quality is the respect between spouses that is based on understanding, mutual respect and the progress of the relationship where the attitude of the husband towards his wife will determine if the marriage is successful or not. Women will always appreciate the husband's sentiments for them, not the sexual life or material life.

The phone conversation between two men is quick before they call back the phone. They know what they need to say and typically call the other person if there's a issue. Once the issue is resolved and the conversation ended, they leave the phone. Women are not the same They can contact their the person they consider to be their best friend for no reason. It's because, as they say that she is eager to converse. Through their tales, women share diverse conversations. It might be possible to call initially since there's something to talk about but from the beginning until the close, the subject has been driving the conversation a dozen times. The clever, "dangerous" way of transferring the subject of gossip between women is more pronounced than when people mix up a pot full of porridge. Perhaps it's the phrase "cooking porridge telephone" is a good place to start!

Men value joy. Women tend to fall in love with those who make their laugh more often however, they will also have the logical perspective of the love of their lives: They seek to find a man who lets their heads sway when they are exhausted, is funny, has a spirit, the ability to help others, and love for the bedroom. While men are less complicated. Men are just looking for an individual who will allow them to unwind, unwind and enjoy themselves with them, without having to pay attention to other matters. A happy wife or girlfriend allows men to open up about their feelings and desire to remain connected for longer durations of time.

Men are attracted by the sex appeal of a woman: For men the primary thing that attracts them to take notice of women is the attraction the woman has, and then they begin to build the feeling of the desire to love. Of of course the more time spent with her to a woman, the more attractive her attractive sex is and men will take a second date when they feel that the woman they are dating is attractive to them. Men must feel attracted by the other before deciding whether or not to go out with her again.

While sitting, men extend their knees in order to prove that they are male. Women do not have to show that since women can be identified by the way they look. Women make funny faces when taking photos with her friends, and a man waits in an inline.

Men were created by God to benefit the entire world. Women were created by God to serve men. In the word "Women" contains the word "men" in it. Men aren't complete without women.

Pets. A woman is a lover of her pet and when she is in front of them the man, he would say "He loves cats too," but when she was turning her back they would kick the pets. Women are more caring than men.

Chapter 4: Confession Versus Discovery

The relationships we have with our partners are usually founded on trust and honesty. We are conditioned to expect that our companions to remain honest every time and that is what they expect from us from them. If there is infidelity, is it appropriate to be honest and confess that to our spouses? We're afraid of what might occur if we did confess because we fear it could end the relationship forever.

The reason you should not reveal your identity is to safeguard your relationship from what might happen. However, is it really a ideal idea to be quiet and not confiding in your spouse? What effect does it have on your relationship? Does it harm or enhance the relationship?

Try putting yourself in the position as your spouse. What would you feel If your partner had cheated on you, but didn't inform you of it? Would you like to know about it or would prefer to stay away from you?

Since relationships are built on trust and honesty and trust, it's best to be transparent with your partner about cheating, rather than let them find out independently. Sharing can ease the burden of guilt. Of course, it will cause the wife to be angry but over the long term it could be the beginning of a stronger bond. It will also create possibility for your partner to share their experience with you that they might be eager to.

Confession is far more effective than letting your partner know about your cheating without telling them. If you keep quiet, it will cause more harm than admitting.

Money, kids or sexual sex are not the only factors that define an ongoing relationship. A long-lasting, happy relationship is based on honesty and trust. This relationship can be damaged when trust is breached and silence is required about infidelity.

A spouse who is cheating will try to keep their affair hidden until they are discovered. This is an obvious sign that guilt is triggered by cheating and that the cheater is aware of the risk that it poses. Cheaters justify their actions by claiming that the things their partner does not know won't harm them. However, keeping secrets from your spouse will harm your relationship. There is a certain degree of physical or emotional anxiety felt by the individual who is being cheated on even though they don't know about the unfaithfulness of their partner. This could even cause the innocent spouse to believe they are the ones to blame for the situation and begin to think of ways to fix the situation without even knowing what the trigger is.

It is therefore the best option to speak to your partner that you have been infidelity and ask the forgiveness of your partner. Restoring trust after a break is the best way of returning your relationship to course after an affair. It's not easy to rebuild trust after a breakup and then be content. It is a matter of telling the truth every day.

Chapter 5: Both Sides In The Story

Love is at the heart of all humankind. Intimacy is regarded as a sign of the love of a marriage and romantic relationships. The need for affection and intimacy is instilled within every human being, whether you are a dreamer, madman doing, or perfect healthy. But these feelings can lead people to their lowest points and can cause an overwhelming sense of emptiness, despair and even sadness. Anyone who has been in love knows how long it can take to get to make someone feel loved. Perhaps, the most difficult part about love is finding out that the person you're in love with may be falling for an individual. The idea that someone we've in love with is likely to be romantically involved with someone else can cause us to be sad in unimaginable ways.

Infidelity can be found all over the world and across many different ways; it is not wise to worry over the thought that you're the only one who is suffering from this kind of loss. It's been happening since the beginning of time and is considered to be a classic however we are not able to condemn it.

As mentioned earlier there are a number of motives for people for cheating on spouses. Most of the time an affair is an external manifestation of something that has been internal that's not quite right for a period of time. In some instances it is the case that infidelity has nothing to do with have to do with the marriage. It is possible for a person to be happily married, but still leave. According to studies the majority of people and women who have strayed from relationships that last a long time revealed that their marriages were happy or extremely happy. What is the reason people cheat in the first place? There are many reasons for people to cheat from their personalities genetics, biological evolution or any other reason. Infidelity, however, is always an option.

The more we know about the root causes of cheating the simpler it will be to heal and move forward. Knowing the root causes of cheating can help to distinguish between infidelity, and the eternal and forever of the relationship.

In the case of cheating, there's the cheater and the victim. If you're the one being victim, remember that the act of infidelity could be unrelated to your relationship or with you personally. It is not your fault what your spouse does and he/she was able to find a better solution instead of cheating. With that in mind it is crucial to examine the relationship in a way that is honest after an affair. Both the cheater and those one who was cheated on must examine the ways in which they could have caused the infidelity. There isn't an adequate motive to commit a crime, and neither is anyone entitled to being victimized However, there are some actions you may have done to push one away. If your spouse was trying to show frustration or sadness, and you were ignoring them and allowing the cheating. It's not your fault that you cheated however neither did your spouse deserve to be ignored.

If you've been open and loving throughout, then cheating won't make sense to you. But, if you'd like to maintain the relationship you must be able for forgiveness and moving on. Be aware that forgiveness doesn't mean that you will forget immediately. It is also not acceptance of what occurred. Forgiving implies understanding enough to prevent emotion and hurt from consuming your life. Humans make mistakes and occasionally, they're very terrible. A few of them could put you on the back foot for a period of time. But , with determination to do so, you will get back on track and continue the relationship.

If you're the one who was a bit off and devoted your love towards someone else than your spouse, it is time to determine if you are ready for the relationship to continue. Examine the causes that led you to wander off. Be accountable for your actions. Be responsible, patient, and show honesty to yourself and your partner. Be compassionate and loving even through the hurt, the frustration, the regret as well as the immense jealousy, until you are able to resolve the issue for good.

One of the most common questions an individual (especially those who have been cheated upon) is likely to ask themselves is whether the cheating resulted in breaking up with the love. Truthfully, anything that involves humans isn't always in black and white. Different people have different personalities, therefore, life can be complex. Humans are complex beings may make a nice person appear like a bad one, and reverse. For example, someone who was cheated on because they felt lost can appear to be someone who is really bad when it was only the first time. The complexity of the relationship can cause love to feel like it's gone for a while so that the person decides to search for that nice sensation outside of the relationship.

The majority of people who have affairs are in fact loving their main partner The majority of people who are having affairs aren't cheaters in nature. If someone were totally in love with their primary partner, they'd quit rather than engage in an additional affair. Certain of the people involved engaged in an affair are not betrayers and liars, so they are not bad individuals. Sure, their actions were not right, but we are all human and has the potential to make terrible mistakes. All of us do it, and will.

The thing I find the most fascinating is that the reason people are engaged in an affair isn't about seeking a new relationship, but rather, it's about wanting to make to make a change in the initial relationship. Every marriage and relationship evolves over time, and as a result our needs could be forgotten. We may forget about things like connection, unconditional love affection, and nurturing when life becomes a mess with other obligations. These issues aren't an acceptable reason who cheat. However, knowing the factors that led to a rift can aid in repairing relationships.

Cheaters will always be caught.

Cheaters are likely to be caught, whether it's the next day, tomorrow, year, or 10 years in the future. The result will not be with a bang. The cheater doesn't have to be caught out with a solid evidence. It could happen in a way the cheater could never have thought of, in a very minute manner, nearly too low. There are a variety of behavior changes which are associated with cheating:

The spouse might begin treating their partner differently or less.

* A wife might alter certain habits for instance exercising more. But, that's not always the case.

* Someone may begin to lie without need.

* It is possible to have unanswered messages and calls.

• Sudden mood changes and moods, as well as other.

There could be valid reasons for these behavior patterns, but when one suspects that something is not quite right An investigation could make it easier to think about the issue. The end result is that the cheater will be discovered due to the nature of it. The effects become too frequent to be concealed. Even when the cheater may have hidden his or her tracks and is caught, the cheater is likely to reach the point of wanting to spend more time. Therefore, it is possible to see numerous calls and messages with no explicit reasons. The emotional conflict that occurs following an affair can be very difficult to ignore.

There's always some indication to the other person that something is not right. Sometimes, the cheater may be able to make himself look good because they are not careful enough. In any case, cheating can cause problems regardless of how clever one is.

The majority of cheaters who is caught cheats multiple times. Someone who cheats once is able to get away with their actions but may confess later in the day because of guilt. People who cheat frequently will at some point in the other end become comfortable, particularly if they've repeatedly done it without getting found guilty. Due to the constant lying, the person who has been deceived might have a difficult time letting go of the cheater. The perpetrator may not apologize for their actions as it has become the normal. A lot of cheating could cause the cheater to be unrepentant and guilt-free. In the absence of guilt or regret the cheater seems not to care about their spouse in any way.

If the culprit does confess, but it is due to guilt and shame the chances are less to be that they have cheated for lengthy. This does not mean that the cheater did not cheat for a long time, but confession can be a great opportunity for forgiveness , particularly when it's coupled with regret, regret, and compassion for the innocent party.

Be sure to keep this principle to keep in mind If a cheater has conscience and a sense of empathy, regret, and compassion for the other is likely to regret the damage done to their relationship and which is why they are more likely to take on building what they did not repair. In the same way, infidelity is not ending your marriage; in fact, it can be a lesson learned from a mistake made. A trustworthy partner will swear never to be in a relationship that is not honest and stick to their promise.

If you've caught your spouse who is cheating and doesn't feel anxious and astonished, regretful and regretful, sorry for hurting youor feeling awful for being caught, then you are likely to be in a wrong relationship. The person may feel guilty because of being caught, but not because of the actions he/she took. Someone who is honest about their pain and guilt over being caught and willing to make amends within the relationship, has greater likelihood of resolving the issue. It will take many things to repair the relationship, but eventually the affair could become an end.

Chapter 6: Why Do Human Beings Cheat?

Unsatisfied with the partners sexually

Men are drawn to experiment, especially with sexuality. They love to experiment and discover their boundaries. Women are, however tend to be more relaxed when it comes to this topic. There is a distinct hunger for sexual desire and if you don't want your spouse to be cheating with you, all you have to find out is whether they're sexually happy with their relationship. If you are able to satisfy this, you may be able stop your partner from making up lies to you. Sexuality is an essential element in most relationships, so you must take this in mind.

Wants to be with other people sexually

Sometimes, one person isn't enough for a person . After many years of being settled an individual suddenly feels the desire to be sexually involved with a different person. The person is looking for some other feeling or is looking for something that is different from his wife. The reason as to the reason he's engaging in an affair with someone else can't be quickly solved. Do you want to let your husband indulge in sexual relations with someone else so you are not romantically connected to the person? If yes you can easily be solved; however, the issue arises when you're not willing to let that happen.

Unsatisfied with the emotional support from a partner

Your spouse is your primary partner in your emotional needs. He is the person that is expected to offer advice, support your heart when you're feeling sad and support you when it appears that everything is against you, and love you with all of their heart. There are instances when your spouse isn't providing the emotional support that you are seeking and you think you have to get help from another person. You might feel the exact as you and may try looking for support from another person. If you are trying to stop him from taking a different direction, then you need to be more understanding and supportive of your friend and let him know that you're enough.

Likes to be appreciated by an individual

Sometimes, your partner is convinced that your love for the work he is doing is not enough. Because you don't convey it in enough ways or he doesn't think about it in any way. It is important to be more expressive. You have to demonstrate to your spouse that you appreciate every single thing you do you value more than ever before. If you truly enjoy it, but it seems that he is seeking more, then it's not a problem for you now, it's just that you think that your appreciation for what you have done isn't enough, and he's looking for more.

I was apathetic and broke up with my the love of

As marriages progress couples lose the enthusiasm they had previously in their spouse. Love is a huge word, and you've both agreed to be together throughout your lives. However, one is never incapable of loving someone else. At some point, perhaps the most difficult time in your relationship, your spouse may discover a different person to love and, as a result they may break up with you. Of course, the affection that he has for you will never cease to be there, but it could be eclipsed by another. When he loses affection for you the only solution is to force him to fall into love with you over and over again.

Will do anything to get back at the other partner

If you've ever been caught cheating with your spouse before and your husband knows about it, there's the possibility that he's doing similar things to you in order to get the same revenge against you. Your spouse wants you to understand how he felt when he saw you cheating and is determined to make you suffer for the act. The best method to retaliate against an individual is to demand an eye that was missing. Since trust is no longer there between you, he is easier to cheat.

Are you looking to experience new things?

There are instances that your spouse is bored with the way you're living. He may be bored and desire to experience new things with a different person. Since marriages tend to stagnate after a certain amount of time It is quite possible that your enthusiasm to explore may diminish while your partner is still looking for excitement, adventure or something similar. If this occurs it is possible that he will look for it elsewhere when it appears you are unable to provide the same.

A lack of intimacy and focus

Do you do the same thing when showing affection the way you used to before? Does time have changed the way you talk to each and touch each other? Do you not have enough time to spend with your spouse and don't give your husband enough time? If you do then you can't blame him for cheating on you. Since the need for intimacy and affection are two of the basic needs that humans have and he wants them from you, his wife. If your relationship isn't able to satisfy these two things, then you can be sure that it to not work out.

Insecurity about oneself

If your spouse isn't confident, you'll need to find someone more confident in himself or her self and capable of standing up for what the person wants. If you are not confident in yourself maintaining your relationship with your spouse might be difficult because you constantly think you're not enough for him and, eventually, he'll become tired of showing yourself that you're worthy of the effort because he is a lover. If you're looking to keep him, but you are not confident in yourself then turn the affection the man has for you into something that can help you believe in your own self.

Financial problems

The issue of money is among the biggest problems in the world and has destroyed several relationships during the last few years. When the husband or wife are unable to provide enough funds for their family, and both parents have children the situation is planned for the most disastrous. It is impossible to live on funds to feed your family, and it isn't easy to keep from loving one another while you're trying to figure out the means to provide for yourself or pay the bills or stop your family from being removed from the home you rent.

The signs that indicate whether your spouse has been cheating

Always dressed up and taking care of your for your physical appearance

Have you noticed a dramatic shift in the style of your loved one? Do you think your spouse is appearing a bit prettier or perhaps with a bit more stylish? Examine the way your partner appears much more elegant than they usually do. If you notice that your person you love is more focused on appearances, he may apply a nice perfume, or buy new clothes, but don't wear them prior to when you. The spouse starts working out more frequently, and is more concerned about his appearance. This should trigger an alarm, particularly when your spouse isn't the kind to do this suddenly. They may try to appear attractive to someone else.

You will spend less time together

Your partner typically comes home late from work or continues to work for longer hours. If you attempt to reach them and inquire about why they'll be late to work or not at all, they usually provide vague explanations or claim that "they could not hear the phone because they're at a meeting or meeting with the business partner"

Get more distant or distracted

If he's always caring or supportive, attuned to you, always close by, asks about your day and loves hanging out with you, he may become engaged in conversations with you about work or life, kids Then they suddenly appear detached or disengaged from you. They might not be interested in family activitiesand rather, they would prefer to be using their mobile or computer. This could be a signal of in a cheating relationship with you.

Protects the computer, phone constantly

If the person you have said you would spend the rest of your days with is constantly looking at the phone or computer to make sure it's far from your reach. If, for instance, you pass by or go into his home, he will tend to switch off the computer or phone immediately. This can be a signal that you be suspicious that he is insecure. It is possible that your partner is keeping things from your. You can't confirm that it's an individual, it could be a huge surprise, but it's certainly suspicious. Even if it is impossible to examine the computer or phone it is worth taking note of.

Remember that you've made a promise to one another that you'll be open about everything, and you might be thinking about the reason your phone is a lot of a security risk. If your partner is keeping some information from you it's generally a negative sign.

Protects everything with an encryption

Apart from calling, do you have something other thing that your spouse appears to be very protective of? You can find out when you borrow the object. For instance, you could borrow someone's laptop. You can claim that you're checking your email, or make an acceptable reason. Make sure that your password is secured.

What's the meaning of all your gadgets in your home that are owned by the person you're involved with are secured by an account with a password? It's possible that the contents could be something that could be a threat to your marriage.

Become defensive

Your partner is uncertain, nervous or defensive when you inquire about his night out or day with friends or with ladies. This could be an indication of cheating.

Are you having arguments with you

A cheating spouse might attempt for you to feel depressed and feel guilty that you did an offense to them. They typically get angry and easily get into arguments, fights or even accuse you of cheating .

New credit cards are issued.

Another indicator that an affair may be taking place is when a credit card is accepted by your spouse. Take a look at what is the reason behind the need for a new credit card you are not able to monitor, other than using it by someone else without notifying you.

This is among the most obvious signs that indicate your spouse is involved in an affair: when funds are spent on an individual you don't know. The more secretive your spouse is more mysterious you'll be.

Starts making hurtful comments

If the love of your life begins to make negative remarks about you, or attempting to brush the incident off as a joke it could be taken as an absence of interest in the relationship. It is even more likely that it could be intentional to make you angry. The most unfortunate thing is that the hurtful or snide remarks could be the real emotions of your spouse.

Always discuss a specific person

If your spouse is prone to introduce a name in conversations, constantly but without motive, even if you don't notice it, there is something terribly wrong. It could be a sign that the person you're talking to is always in your partner's thoughts. A mistake in speech is the most common way criminals are found guilty. So, if that special person keeps mentioning an individual's name, and telling stories of this person, be aware that this could be someone to be wary of.

Disseminates negative remarks about a particular person

If, by chance, you have a loved one who is scathing about someone and you think that this is intentionally, you should reconsider. The negative comments you make about a certain person could be a sign of covering up any evidence of affection. Don't let this fool you. You should be cautious about your spouse and ensure that the person you are talking to you and the other spouse and not in any romantic relationship. Do your best to inquire for information or inquire to verify your suspicions.

It suggests separate holiday celebrations

Couples generally spend their holidays with each other because they view it as a time to bond at least in part. For instance, if your spouse suggests you take separate holidays, it could result in him having the holiday with an individual. It's best to not let your spouse know about this and observe how he will react. If he is angry and becomes agitated at the time of the holiday, you've proven that your spouse may be being involved with someone else.

Doesn't need physical intimacy

Sexual intimacy is an essential aspect of marriage and, sometimes, it's one of the factors that binds a relationship. If your spouse always comes up with a reason not to have sexual relations with you, this ought to be cause for alarm. In the end, being in the decision to love your partner is a sign that you share a love between you. What are the main reasons why that your spouse isn't willing to be in love with you in the future? One reason could be that he's having an affair and getting the sexual pleasure he desires with a different person and doesn't feel the need to share the same thing with you. It could be that they are less romantic or intimate or be able to feel as distant when they are having sexual relations. Your partner may not give you a hug , or a kiss. Perhaps you don't want him to touch you like the way he used to.

Social media is a great place to flirt.

Social media is definitely one of the best methods to determine whether your spouse is involved in an affair. A majority of the time people don't bother the privacy of their lives from their accounts on social media, therefore the signs of an affair could be evident when you attempt to find out. You can look for someone who constantly likes your spouse's pictures or comments on them or perhaps posting something on their wall. It could indicate that he's having an affair with someone else or they're connected.

Of of course, these are only indicators to let you know whether your spouse is involved in unfaithful relations or is not. There is a chance that it could be a mistake however, if you have all the indications you may want to take a closer look.

Learnings from the incident

After all the difficulties, there are a lot of lessons you've taken away from the experience. Being aware that your partner is lying to you could be difficult thing to accept, however, it can teach you many lessons. Here are some lessons you could learn from the experience.

Infidelity is not the blame.

It's not your blame that your husband chose to look for a new partner to be with and smear sweet words. However, if your marriage is not working there is a chance that you have made a few errors as well. As much as you'd like not to blame your partner it is not possible. there is a small portion of the blame. But, in the end cheating was his choice and one that which he had made on his own and that's the truth.

The moment you learn about an affair can change the way you view it.

The knowledge that your husband has cheated you takes a small piece of your heart and will never be found. It can change your life and make you feel as if you're not enough and that you'll not be sufficient for any other person. He chose a different person instead of you, even though he said he would always choose you, and it will leave a mark on your heart that nobody will be capable of erasing. Don't worry, you're a tough woman and you can overcome this something you'll be able to do.

It is necessary to let him go if he wishes to be released

If you catch him the first thing he's likely to do is to ask forgiveness, especially in the event that you've been anything other than a great husband to him. Unfortunately, there are instances when a husband requests to be let go. Don't be a victim of this, but be aware that you have to decide if you want to allow him to go or not. It is best to let him go and tell him that no matter what the man has done you are still adamant about the fact that he's your husband. The love you feel for him is enough to allow him to go.

The forgiveness will eventually come

Another thing you'll take away from the incident is that in the end healing will occur, and you will be capable of allowing your husband to be forgiven for the acts you did to him. It is a long, lengthy time, but forgiveness will be forthcoming. It won't take you by surprise but it will be like tiny waves that rush to your heart. If you love him still and would like him to be by your side as the moment of forgiveness swells your heart.

It is more beneficial to leave things by yourself rather than be taken advantage of

While forgiveness may occur, the trust that you've established will remain broken , and it's extremely difficult to maintain an untrusting relationship. Be aware that if you believe there is a chance that he will ever again cheat on you If you truly want to let him go, as it's better to be in peace than to let him go at it repeatedly until you don't understand the reason for inviting him back to you.

Chapter 7: The Reasons To Be Hurt When You Are Being Cheated

Violation of Expectations

When you begin the relationship, you enter into it with a set of expectations about what is expected to happen in a relationship. This includes romantic, emotional and sexual loyalty to each other.

But, when a partner commits a bribe and you are not satisfied, they breach your expectations. This is especially painful since it is from someone whom you trusted.

Feelings of resistance

The feeling of being cheated changes your life significantly. It causes a sudden and unwelcome change in your life.

It's something you need to address as you blame the partner for it and wish them to resolve the issues since they are at fault. You are an aggressor while you wait for the issues to be resolved.

Be afraid that you'll suffer for the rest of your life.

If you've been the victim is hurt, it's natural to feel fear especially in the case of a partner. The constant feeling of hurting makes people feel even more wounded.

But, you must to be strong and push forward.

Robbed past

If you've been scammed on, you begin to doubt everything you were told about the previous. You begin to doubt everything you have heard from the past. It makes you feel as if you've been robbed of your memories of the past.

Feeling of guilt

If you've been duped on, you are wondering if your partner would have stayed away from doing the same thing if you were to have done things in a different manner.

Chapter 8: Effects Of Betrayal To Our Brain

Sexual intimacy is an extremely delicate subject following an affair, particularly for innocent partners. You're desperate to be physically connected with your loved one however, you must not allow your wall of safety and security in your emotional life fall. Who wants to be injured and again, particularly with the vulnerability that sexual intimacy demands?

You might feel self-conscious about the way you look in comparison to the lover of your partner. You might be suffering with anxiety over your performance, and wonder if you'll please your partner more than his partner. With your dramas, you might struggle to be excited about intimacy.

When your loved one truly loves you, he'll be able to understand the anxieties and worries you're feeling. You should both be honest about your expectations of intimacy, passion and fears of intimacy.

It is likely that you're not hooked to a selfish and demanding spouse who thinks that your job is to be pleasing him. A romantic relationship will only flourish when both partners are genuinely concerned about each other's concerns and desires. For the guys out there it is impossible to have sexual intimacy with a woman until her emotional needs are satisfied. This is the reason you need to address their emotional demands of one the other before you can begin to talk about your own needs. Men are generally not in touch with their emotions However, I can assure that if you focus on communicating your emotions to your partner she will cherish you to the core. Achieving your emotional needs first will lead to amazing sexual intimacy.

Set the tone for intimacy sexually in the early hours of the day with activities that increase emotional intimacy. Concentrate on meeting the other's needs, and helping one another. If you are focused on meeting your partner's emotional needs, she'll become more willing to fulfill your sexual desires.

In regards to sexual preferences and sexual needs It is crucial that you each communicate your needs and preferences, as well as what you find uncomfortable. If you're having fantasies you want to share, do it with your partner. When you do this Don't set unreasonable expectations or expectations for your partner (like your partner must already have everything you need to achieve). Make sure you communicate them in a caring manner and pay attention to how well your partner will be with the desires. Do not force your partner to satisfy your sexual desires without regard to their self-esteem and beliefs. If you do, it will cause friction between you and your partner and also impede any healing processes. Should you find that your significant other and you have issues in this area I would suggest seeking assistance from a skilled sexual therapy therapist.

If you adhere to these principles of respect and tender care of each other's needs you'll be able to build a fulfilling and exciting sex relationship together.

Chapter 9: Feelings Of Jealousy And Anger

Jealousy

Jealousy can be described as the unpleasant feeling that occurs when an intruder invades something they believe is theirs. It can be difficult and even difficult to discuss with a spouse or with anyone. In general it is typically associated with romantically engaged couples, however it could occur in any relationship, and can cause emotions of distress and even conflict. Most cultures promote monogamous relationships. Jealousy tends to arise because of suspicions or fears that one person isn't loyal or is not loyal anymore. The feeling of jealousy can hamper the ability of an individual to communicate if not dealt with appropriately. If communication isn't clear and effective couples could even misinterpret the intentions or expectations of one another about the relationship. What is acceptable to one person may be dangerous to their relationship for the other and without clear communication nobody will be able to discern the limits. The perception of culture about infidelity influences how jealousy is displayed. Most of the time women are expected to be tolerant of their husbands even when cheating. However women are slammed as well as shamed and assessed harshly.

According to research the concept of jealousy is not easy to define in its own however it is characterized by difficult feelings like abandonment, loss, betrayal or embarrassment, anger, or even shame. Modern research has revealed an interaction with the brain's attachment system in your brain as well as the primitive characteristic of jealousy. This attachment mechanism is essential in social bonding , and it will react when confronted by external dangers. In light of this it is possible to say that jealousy is a fundamental negative force that can be a catalyst for the growth of a relationship , and prevents the temptation to commit infidelity.

But, not all types of jealousy are good for you. Certain research studies showed that excessive jealousy is associated with instability. People who are overly jealous tend to be less friendly and are emotionally unstable. That means that overly jealous individuals will attempt to influence their spouses' lives by observing the people they hang out with, and what they wear and look for ways to weaken their self-esteem.

It is often difficult to manage jealousy, particularly if there's no reason for the feeling. The majority of the time, unneeded jealousy stems from feelings of being inadequate. Recent research in psychology have shown that many people seek to convey their frustration on others by showing anger and, consequently, the need to control their relationship as much as is possible. However, one of the partners may feel overwhelmed and will look for ways to ease the pressures of their relationship. A lot of jealousy can cause more harm than good.

Gender and Jealousy

According to research conducted in Chapman University about infidelity, women and men differ in their approach to jealousy. The study involved nearly 64,000 Americans studying the reactions of different genders to infidelity (sexual and. emotional infidelity). It was discovered that heterosexual males were more upset over intimate relationships than homosexual females. But, men tend to be less unhappy about emotional infidelity when relative to women.

Infidelity both emotional and sexual can lead to harm for both women and men as well as abrupt termination of relationships, heartache that leads to violence as well as loss of resources or broken relationships. The reactions of the partners to threats of infidelity entailed intense jealousy and even an elaborate displays of affection in attempts to win back the partner who was straying. In the case of jealousy, it can result in aggressive and selfish behavior, consequently, it is crucial to know the most powerful factors that trigger jealousy.

Infidelity and jealousy are usually linked. If you think that another person poses an issue to the relationship you have with them, then jealousy will creep into. Research has shown that jealousy is associated with fear of losing, anger and distrust due to the fact that the person is scared of losing the relationship due to an adversary. Usually, jealousy serves as an instrument by which people are vigilant to guard the relationship from unwelcome intruders. The most common situation that can trigger jealousy happens when a spouse is confronted by someone who is threatening, resulting in the perception that the person could be unfaithful.

There are many theories about infidelity and each offers an explanation. If we examine social role theories versus evolutionary psychologists, you will notice distinction in how distress is assessed. The evolutionary psychologists are focussed on forced choices in which the respondents are forced to choose the option they find most troubling. The options involve emotional infidelity. This is where the spouse is emotionally connected to another person without being in a relationship of physical or emotional infidelity, where the spouse is physically close to someone without necessarily becoming emotionally connected. This has shown that men are more irritated over the physical (sexual infidelity) and females are much more likely be irritated by emotional infidelity.

From an evolutionary standpoint from an evolutionary perspective, gender differences result in different responses to infidelity. According to this view, women are afraid that if men are emotionally involved with other women, they'll be deprived of the resources they have from men. In contrast, males worry that women might be sharing their resources with men who were not involved in the gathering of the resources. Both genders are worried about the resources they have and who they can reach. This is why jealousy can arise.

But, not everyone is with this view. Some believe that the differing opinions result from the manner in which questions are asked. If everyone was given a opportunity to express their opinion instead of choosing between two choices, the outcomes could be different. We can however look at it by looking at the evolutionary angle and discover the real cause of debates about jealousy and possessions. It could have been a the result of challenges to resources and a couple may not have enough to meet their requirements and consequently be seeking to shield the child they have from intrusion. In such a scenario the male partner could be more concerned about sexual relationship infidelity when it is suspected that the child being carried by the woman isn't his.

However women are more envious if they believe that their hard-earned wealth is being diverted to other individuals instead of their own children. Therefore, women are more envious when they believe there is a possibility that the person has formed relationships with another person since there is a risk of resource redistribution.

It is important to find methods to get rid of these agitated emotions and emotions. Communication with a loved anyone to resolve any miscommunications. If the suspicions are valid, the couples can find a solution to resolve their issue without resorting to jealousy and its results. If communication is not reliable couples have a slim chance of understanding the viewpoint of one another. If jealousy turns into a significant issue that affects the quality of the relationship counselling could help. In a counseling session the couple will benefit from a professional counsellor who will devote time to find a solution for the issue.

Is there a reason to be jealous?

Research suggests that a touch of jealousy can be beneficial to relationships, particularly when couples are still in the beginning stages. The trust level isn't yet established in the beginning of the relationship. Thus, a little bit of jealousy could be a sign and encourage the commitment. A moderate amount of jealousy is typically viewed as a sign of love, and can determine if it's appropriate to continue investing into the relationships. When a partner makes use of jealousy to demonstrate the importance of loyalty and commitment, the other partner is reassured that they are investing into the marriage.

Vengeance

The most devastating things that can happen in a marriage or relationship is discovering that your spouse who you have a great faith in and hoped to for your entire life with, is being a cheater. You are hurting bleeding and in complete angst.

The infidelity of the spouse or partner can trigger the same kind of anger from the partner who is snubbed and triggers the desire to get revenge. If the spouse decides to accept the apology or take on the issue with vengeance depends on the external and internal elements. Experts believe that the desire to cut some tires or throw a cell phone out of the window is a deep-seated instinct. It is a primitive impulsive behavior. It's more of an aggressive retaliation strategy to shield ourselves from being taken advantage of. In general, revenge is intended to stop those who are stealing from you. So when someone hits you, you will punch back. The instinct to protect serves as a deterrent to keep others from harming you. But, revenge or revenge can go wrong.

When someone discovers that their partner is cheating, a sense of anger is created and areas of the brain such as the ventralstriatum and the amygdala first react. The amygdala is aware of the danger, while the ventral striatum , in conjunction with the nucleus acumens records the satisfaction it feels of retribution. The more advanced area of the brain known as the prefrontal cortex that is accountable for self-control and social behavior, intervenes. If this section of the brain is not functioning as it should due to one reason or another like an inability to eat, an injury or lack of sleep or intoxication, or any other kind deficiency, then the individual is more likely to resist the desire to take revenge. The research also shows that in certain people more communication is not happening between the brain's prefrontal cortex and other brain regions which means that people are more likely to take revenge.

Researchers have discovered that the satisfaction of revenge is higher when it's done against a partner who is romantically involved. This may be the reason that most people are motivated to take revenge once they realize that their spouse has been cheating on them. While there aren't any scientific evidence to suggest that revenge is likely to be more enjoyable against an ex-partner but experts have discovered that both genders tend to feel the urge to revenge on the same levels. But, men are more likely to take action in pursuit of revenge, when compared to women, and are more likely to cause damage when they are angry. A significant portion of home violence involves men beating their wives as a way of retribution for infidelity, whether real or imagined. This is why it is necessary to conduct more investigation into why revenge seems to be a good feeling in the event of infidelity.

Retaliation and revenge cheating are the most common choices when spouses discover that their partner has cheated. Most men will use violence against their spouses when they discover that their wife is involved having extramarital affairs, and they might decide to get out, while women opt for retaliation. If a hurt partner decides to respond, they feel justified. Some of these spouses who are hurt are capable of identifying someone they believe will cause total ruin to the cheating spouse. It could be a friend or colleague, a business rival, or an individual from the family. Some spouses will ensure that the cheater is aware of their cheating, even if it means that they have to catch them in the act.

The belief is that cheating should cause the cheater to be humiliated as much as it does the person who is cheating. It's usually meant to teach the person who is cheating to learn. But, it's important to note that retaliation rarely will yield the desired results.

Retaliation and revenge can be extremely dangerousand, rather than hurting the guilty partner, they can ruin the chances of healing of the relationship. Instead of the spouses coping with the issue that is infidelity they wind being faced with multiple issues, which complicate the situation. The result is usually tragic and leaves the couple hurt or worse.

There are a variety of reasons any spouse should not engage in infidelity-related actions with the intent of retribution:

Retaliation affairs destroy relationship recovery.

If a spouse discovers the other spouse is cheating and then engages in a plan to retaliate They are disengaged from the primary motive behind the cheating. People are focused on retribution the other party, and they do not consider the possibility of solving the issue in a comprehensive manner. If a relationship has was affected due to an incident the relationship is at risk. Retribution and revenge could only make matters worse. In the end there will be more doubts as a result lies and betrayal and the couple are likely to fall further apart. In essence, retaliation can fuel an already hot fire.

Inflicting retribution or revenge could stifle your recovery.

Finding out that a spouse has been cheating can leave one feeling slighted, rejected and abused. The idea of retaliation may appear to be the best option but it's not a solution that works. Retribution will only increase the feelings of disapproval and anger coupled with guilt and hurt, making the person who is hurt feel even more devastated. It is essential for everyone to confront their own feelings on a personal basis or with the assistance of counselors. Retribution is not the answer. facing the pain is to be in denial and can only hinder any healing.

Retaliation for infidelity will only damage your image.

When you take everything into consideration Retaliation is unnatural and serve as the possibility of coping mechanisms, which typically is retrograde and serves only you. Retribution is simply a method of expressing anger and getting back with your partner with a childish attitude. It shows a variety of mistakes and is not doing anyone any good. Instead, it degrades the foundations of your relationship you've constructed over the course of many years.

Retaliation is only going to get you into the blame game.

Typically, cheating partners will blame the innocent spouse if discovered. This could mean you are no longer grooming well, you're too busy to attend to my needs, or you're not attractive or approachable anymore or whatever reason that they believe to be acceptable. A retaliation based on infidelity can only give the cheater another reason to blame you for the crime. In the eyes of your cheating partner you're already at fault so why give him or her another reason to accuse you?

Whatever you decide to take, retaliation won't succeed. The best way to retaliate is to succeed. Be sure to win at whatever you wish to. Make an effort to overcome the challenges while simultaneously ensure that you are successful in everything you do. You are entitled to flourish and succeed.

We are wired to seek revenge when we do wrong However, as we've previously mentioned, seeking revenge on the cheating partner will not help you. In fact, it hinders you from healing the hurts. Therefore, it is crucial to stop our angry thoughts before they transform into regrettable acts. The chances of healing are better if we stop our need to play tit to get the sake of.

How can you channel your anger energy?

Do your best.

The old saying goes doing the right thing is the best way to get back. Concentrate all your efforts on becoming a better person. Try to be a person that your cheater is able to feel the pain of losing. You'll not only recover faster and feel more confident in yourself, but will inspire anyone who is aware of what's going on in the background. The more mature reactions are more likely to prevail in this kind of case. Keep in mind that cheating spouses tend to transfer the blame onto innocent partners. Be determined to meet your personal goals, achieve your happiness and improve. Learning playing the piano as well as get back to your best will bring you more joy than just imagining how you'll take care of the toilet using the brush of the culprit.

Create.

In the moment when you feel victimized, deceived and possibly snubbed Your first goal should be to repress the desire to get revenge. It is important to find ways to put aside the narrative that is in the forefront and suffocating your heart. This can be achieved by letting yourself feel the pain and loss before directing that energy towards making. Find a task that is stimulating your body and mind like cooking or drawing, writing or making. Creativity is a therapeutic force and, when one is engaged within it, their mind is free from pain immediately.

You're in charge.

The spouse who was cheating with you is not in any influence over your emotions. Only you are the person who has the power to let the person to control you. In the absence of that, you are in control of your thoughts, words and actions. When you realize that, it becomes difficult for those who are causing trouble to follow over you. It is easier to adhere to the values that you cherish, such as non-violence and forgiveness. Knowing that you are in control of your own life, you will be able to remain within your limits. If you are thinking about the hurt you've felt and the way to get revenge turn your attention towards positive thoughts. Rememberthat you have the power.

Choose to accept forgiveness.

Infidelity is emotionally devastating for the majority of people. It isn't easy to forgive someone who has violated your trust, nor is it easy to get over the agonizing emotional pain that comes with infidelity. However, it is easy to make progress towards this issue and defeat the urge to retaliate. There is no need to work towards reconciliation, nor do you need to forget about the hurtful act. However, you must recognize it is the nature of your partner and that he/she has made a wrong decision that was not weighed with thought. In this way, you'll be able to shift toward a better perspective. The retribution you receive could have disastrous consequences. It is possible that you be in the courtroom or even in jail for destruction of the property of someone else. If you take these consequences into consideration it is best if you refrain from taking revenge to let the issue go.

Chapter 10: From Healer To Destroyer

Accept your feelings

The first thing you must do is accept your feelings and yourself. Accept that you've been injured. Only after you recognize and accept that you're hurt and suffering from pain is it possible to work to fix the issue. The process of healing will begin when you reach this point. Keep your eyes on the prize. There is no rush to express your emotions. It's fine to let your emotions out and cry your emotions. Make a pillow your pillow if you need to. Shout out every occasionally and a good scream could be very therapeutic. Be sorry for what's transpired. It's entirely your responsibility. Accept your responsibility If you have any, but then accept the blame and forgive yourself. Focus on the ultimate objective, which is recovering and moving forward.

Have a serious look at your own self

A little reflection at this point could be beneficial. Have a look at your. Do you have any habits that you'd like to change? Perhaps there were some mistakes that you made during your relationship that led to the breakup. It could be the perfect time to correct these issues. This will allow you to develop and improve yourself. This will ultimately aid in creating better lives.

Don't hesitate to ask for help

Separation is a difficult moment. Don't forget that, and don't be reluctant to seek out help. Anyone you know might be feeling sorry for you, however, people don't necessarily know how to respond. There's a chance that a lot of people are scared they'll cause you to feel even worse. People who are friends with you may stop inviting them over as they aren't sure which of them to invite. If this happens, seeking help from a professional to get you through this painful time might be a viable alternative. Speak to a counselor about your feelings of anger or sadness. You'll discover that you feel better about the situation. There's no reason not to consider seeking help from a professional. Don't let any negative beliefs stop you from seeking help.

Forgive and forget

This could be a difficult decision to make when you've been deceived. Resentment can be an unpleasant emotion. Resentment and anger can only cause you to experience more hurt. Make an effort to forgive yourself and let it go. Forgetting does not necessarily mean you'll be out of your thoughts. It's simply let go. Take the lead. That's the most effective method to get ahead.

Find what makes you happy.

There are many dreams that you've dreamed of as a child. Review your desires. You may find things you let slide by the wayside due to a variety of reasons. Take a look at those things. It is possible that you have things that you'd like to complete quickly. Perhaps you've had always wanted how to swim or pursue an economics degree. Take a look. It will be clear the importance of these issues and being successful at these things will increase confidence in yourself. Be aware of the future. Remember that you're perfectly in good shape before the time they entered your life. Your happiness is not dependent on someone else. It is based on you.

Find new passions

Something fresh to distract your mind will get rid of the negative thoughts in your mind. It could be dancing or art or simply walking. Spend a few minutes each week to indulge in this new passion. If it's an activity that you haven't indulged together, it can aid in taking your thoughts off of them all the time.

Avoid being alone

The most harmful thing you can do when grieving is to be in solitude. Be more active. Visit your acquaintances. Take a group class. Join an online support group. If all else fails, do some window shopping. If you are alone, it will cause you to be a bit solitary. Set a schedule in which you are spending a specific portion of the day in company of other people.

Discover how to be a part of your personal company

While it is beneficial to connect with others and not be in a lonely place in times of depression It is also beneficial to get to know your own business.

It is possible to begin with small amounts in the beginning If you are struggling. Take a moment to relax in silence. Perhaps you can take advantage of a peaceful spot in the in the open air. Find a way to relax and have positive thoughts as you practice this.

Exercise

Exercise that is vigorous and intense releases endorphins. The hormones known as endorphins help you feel great. Also, you'll enjoy the benefit of being fit and healthy. If you're going through a break-up the chance of developing health issues is very high. You'll be experiencing low moods and the likelihood is that you'll be skipping meals. Training will ensure that you stay fit and fit and healthy.

Set goals

Set goals for yourself. Create plans for the future. Set out to reach your goals. Aiming for the future is an excellent method to motivate yourself. It is possible that you feel you've lost your way since you've lost the vision you imagined together, but this isn't how things should go. It is important to concentrate on making your life better with goals and setting them is ideal way to accomplish it.

Work on your self-esteem

Don't be too critical of yourself. Work at your self-esteem. Nothing is more depressing that believing that this is all your responsibility. Recovery will be difficult if you are losing your self-esteem. It's not the fault of you.

Try volunteering

Volunteer for a cause. Being able to help those who are less fortunate than yourself can be uplifting. In one way, you see there are people who have more trouble than you. When you are focused on their problems you begin to feel less. If people are being helped, they're likely to be extremely nice to you. It will definitely feel good. Human beings are the best.

Talk with your buddies

First thing that you should do to get all your sadness, anger fear, and mixed emotions under the right track can be to allow them flow. Chat it out with your loved ones so that the heightened emotions diminish. The best way to get back on track is to express your true feelings and allow your friends to advise you on what you need to do, or allow them to sympathize with you to give you the courage to face another day knowing that what you have learned that the incident was averted will be a shock to you.

Be sure to ask all questions you have

If you have a disagreement with your spouse or your husband and ask them all questions you'd like to find out about the incident that they were involved in. The answers to all the questions that pop up in your head can help you be able to get past the incident and will make you feel more confident about your own. If nothing else is bothering you, getting settled and becoming more calm and strong will be a lot easier. It requires courage to find the truth and make them feel that you're willing to take the risk. Don't be afraid by the possibility that the person they replaced you with could be prettier , and you will be more confident in yourself.

Keep calm throughout the entire process

When the incident is over and your spouse or husband is on the floor asking forgiveness, settle down. Don't show any emotion such as fear, or despair, not even the slightest bit of anger or satisfaction. Allow them to feel the weight of what they've caused you to feel. Be calm throughout the entire process, even when you tell them that you'll allow them to try again, and to fix the mistakes they created.

Schedule a time for discussion about the incident.

In order to heal from the incident it is essential to acknowledge that it took place. It is important to know the length of time it has been in the making and the details of the incident. You've been asking all the questions you'd like to ask, but setting an exact time frame so you are able to discuss the incident would be better. Make a set time, approximately 15 to 20 minutes per day to discuss the event and only that.

Be prepared for the release of emotions

It is not realistic to expect your spouse to be as serene the way you do. You should be prepared for the possibility that he may unleash feelings at you, and he may suddenly collapse during your fights. It is important to recognize that he's human, as well and when defending himself there could be emotional outbursts you have be aware of. Be sure to ensure that the person isn't overdoing it and does not harm you .

Inform your partner about what happened to you.

You won't try to get revenge, but rather in order to remain fair and fair. It is imperative to let them know what you thought about the instances that they did cheat on you, and especially in when you realized that you had caught them engaging in the act. Be honest about your story and be as truthful as you can. Don't exaggerate to cause your spouse or husband to be more burdened. Tell them in the most straightforward way you can that the situation that they were involved in has had a profound impact on you in a variety of ways . It has also changed how you view them, how you view them, and the impact it has had upon your loved ones.

Do not be quick to forget your spouse

If your spouse was asking for forgiveness from you while they were on their knees, it is right to you to apologize to your spouse or husband. They have still cheated on you and that's a fact. Make them aware that you're mad at them for the wrongs that they did and that they have to come clean to you. Be wary of being swayed even when they claim to be able to tell you things you would like to be told. Remember that these are unsubstantiated promises till they prove real. Inform them of this and let your spouse or husband think about what they have committed wrong.

Take time to spend time with him and not talking about the relationship.

It is only possible to recover from an incident if you don't have it constantly on your mind. Avoid talking about the incident whenever you're with your spouse. Enjoy your time with him as you did before, going dining out, watch films, attend gatherings and other events. You must inform him that even though you aren't ready to forgive the man yet but there is a possibility that you will.

That is all he has to do to be able to hold onto to save your relationship from ending.

Chapter 11: Learning To Forgive

For those who have been cheated on some people may suggest that all you need to do is accept the apology and it will be okay however, you are aware well that it is more difficult to do than it is said and that there's no way to forgive in a way that is easy. They are, however, correct. If you want for your marriage to be saved and begin the next chapter of your lives You must be able to be willing to forgive. By forgiving you can stop judging your spouse for every small thing he or she does, and you begin trusting them again. When you forgive you let yourself let go of the past and demonstrate an eagerness to make a fresh start.

If you're the one who has made a mistake in damaging their loved ones for forgiveness, it is also an important factor. Who should you accept forgiveness from? Yourself. If things go south and you blame yourself and your past mistakes and instead of rescuing your relationship, you'll become a victim of it. The constant guilt that you feel from the past can lead to lower self-esteem, and you could let your partner become the one who is "always the right one" even though it's not due to fear of having to hurt them again. This isn't a healthy relationship. That's why it's essential to be able to forgive yourself Yes, you made an error but this doesn't mean you aren't able to make amends. Sure, you committed a mistake, but this doesn't mean that you're required to be feeling guilt-ridden all the time, regardless of whether it was your responsibility. Instead of dwelling on the guilt that comes from this error, consider absorbing the lessons learned from this error. By doing this, you're not just making yourself more successful as well as helping to improve the quality of your relationship by becoming stronger and more successful as a partner.

If your partner has informed you that he's going to do all will be in his power to convince your that he's grown and that he will remain the trustworthy friend he used to be. Would you be willing to risk your life and allow him to try again? Is love any less sweet this time around? Every person deserves another chance to prove that they are worthy, and you should be sure to let him take a different perspective on your relationship. Here are a few ways to give your cheating spouse another chance.

Strategies to consider when you are giving your spouse who is cheating another chance

You've had your spouse making you that they will never leave you and you're enthralled to it, yet you carry around lots of doubts. So this second chance is an opportunity to test the waters of forever together. Here are some options you could test out to give the relationship a second chance.

Find a nice place to go to enjoy a relaxing holiday

Escape from the location in which the cheating took place and anything that can remind your friend and you of that scandal. Travel to somewhere far away or somewhere with a lovely landscape for an out of season getaway. Perhaps you could go to the beach or out in the countryside, around the world with him and rekindle the romance that you had previously. Maybe on your vacation you'll realize that you really love each other and forget about the romance that occurred.

Let him pamper you

If he would like to treat you like a queen, he can cook to you for your pleasure, kiss your every morning as he gets up and brings you breakfast in the morning, choose your outfit for you, kiss you whenever you're able to, take your coat and help you get settled in your chair, and help you carry your luggage, and let him. Make him feel as a queen, because you are one of them and are worthy of it. This could be the way to say that you are sorry and the repentance is his own. This could be a way to tell that he loves you despite all. Let him show you that he's changed and that having a second affair is extremely unlikely to occur in the future.

Don't judge him/her.

If the person you are with isn't right to you, don't be harsh with them. Let them have the right to choose what they wish to do. And demonstrate to them that you cherish them and value the work they've done to help you. It is not possible to continue to judge them throughout the duration of your life because of one error they committed and then forget all the good things they've accomplished.

Stop assuming he is a threat

There is nothing good that is born of suspicion. If you really want to give him another chance, then forget about the incident ever took place. He is free to do the things he believes will be beneficial for him, but don't be a slave to his every step. Be sure to not be constantly monitoring his emails and messages. Offer him the benefit doubt each time you suspect he's cheating again. You're doing this to keep your relationship intact and to believe that he's able to make a change, and take the initiative and let you take care of yours.

Rekindle your love over again

It's not like that your love has gone away because that he was cheating on you and your love is still there, but your trust is only a less secure. Consider What is the most effective method you can use to offer him another chance without having to be a snob? Easy enough, all you have to do is to get over him once more. You will fall in love with his efforts to make amends to you, and in the way he does to convince you that he's still worth you , and how the man he was on chose to stay by your side.

Keys to repair things

If you've made the decision that you want to give him having another shot, all that is left to do is patch things together and return to the bond you once shared. Here are some ways to relax and bring a smoother ride in your relationship.

Talk to someone.

Discuss the experiences you've been through. Let him know how you noticed that he had changed his behavior and how you are glad to see him keep his word now. Tell him how much you are grateful that he decided to remain with you and preserve your marriage. It's not an easy decision and he chose to deal in that, rather than taking the easy road to get out.

Find out how you can create a relationship that works for you.

After you've had that discussion, you could be able to decide the best way to keep your relationship going. Do you want to go back to how you were before or are you able to make an opportunity to start over? Listen to his perspective as well Don't just keep talking about the things you would like to see take place. Make sure you are a part of the team taking this decision since you're still married at the end of the day.

Don't think about it

Inform him that the matter isn't important to you at the moment so long as you make a promise to never repeating the same thing. And then, you can completely forget about the matter, erase it from your memory and go in your relationship like nothing ever occurred and continue being together in blissful harmony.

In the end Everyone deserves to be given a second chance, and it's never too late to grant the opportunity to him. If he chose you, then he has to keep his commitments and making sure that you're satisfied. He has the right to prove his worth to you, at most and that's why he should.

Chapter 12: Rebuilding Trust

The word "trust" refers to the complete faith in a person. It takes a lot of faith in the belief that the person you trust will not harm you in any way or intentionally hurt you.

Make sure you trust your partner with complete confidence. This will only happen by being more understanding and are able to understand each one another. Maintain your confidence by not sharing all that goes on in your relationships with people. There may be a close friend that you've known for a long time, but when you start an intimate partnership, the person you are with has to be your closest partner. Do not share the secrets of your life with your close friends. Always take into consideration your spouse's requirements and preferences when you make any decision. If you are unsure, inquire before you make a decision.

Never make promises you are unable to keep. When you make a promise and you've made it a point to keep it up with it. This is among the most important factors to build confidence.

You can share things about you from your experiences in the past. Refraining from sharing things with you partner, or remaining indecent is not going to help create trust. It is evident that this cannot be done on a single-handed basis and must be handled in the interests of both spouses.

Life can be full of twists and turns. There will be both ups and downs. It is important to believe in one another and this can be achieved with plenty of open communication and respect. Always remain supportive of each other. If there are disagreements between you and your partner's parents, ensure that even if it isn't yours to share the viewpoint of your partner that you express your disagreement just in private. Do not criticize or argue with your partner in front of other people.

In order for your spouse to recover from an incident You must ensure that you have feasible ways to restore the relationship that was already damaged. Finding strategies for rebuilding will help your spouse gain back trust and confidence in you, so you can be able to move on with ease. There is no need to avoid it, but It may be difficult to overcome the issue. This is especially true when you attempt to help your spouse to get over the loss. It is possible to get the impression that this incident will disappear completely. But, this isn't going to make a difference and you must be persistent and devise strategies to rebuild that demonstrate to your partner that you have a commitment to her or him and you are willing to remain together for the long haul.

Rebuilding your faith in your relationship after an affair can be done but it isn't easy in the same way. It could be overwhelming and require longer than you think to make sure that your spouse is totally healed. An affair could have negative consequences for your marriage and may be a stressful experience for you both. The reactions you might notice from your partner range from surprise, sadness, confusion or despair, as well as anger as well as other emotions that are negative. It's important to understand that rebuilding your relationship after been involved in an incident is a procedure that involves denial and anger, as well as shock as well as acceptance and forgiveness.

In the event of being into an affair, and violating the vows of your marriage or relationship In doing this, the fundamental components of the relationship, such as honor, commitment and trust can be broken. If your partner is aware you've been involved in an affair, it causes them to question their views about their relationship as well as the perception they hold about their partner. If you are involved in your partner in an affair, the security of your marriage is compromised. There are a myriad of re-building steps you can follow in order to make sure that you spouse is free of the hurt that was caused by your error. To help you build trust, here are a few suggestions to aid you.

Strategies for building a solid, trusting connection

Do not rush through the process.

Doing your best to speed up the process of healing is one of the errors to avoid. If you've been involved in an affair, do not attempt to pressure your spouse out of the mess or prevent them from speaking about the incident. It is important to realize that your spouse may be suffering and grieving because of the incident. It is important to note that once you have come to the discovery that you've had been involved in an affair, you partner suffers an untreated wound. So, you are not able to treat the wound simply by plapping it on or applying the bandage hoping the wound will heal. You must develop a long-term treatment that does not offer a quick fix for the issue.

If you think that you don't want to address the issue, or have attempted for a long period of time to get your spouse heal, does not mean that you can't pressure them to resolve the issue. It may seem to you that it is something that is over, but for your spouse, it could remain still fresh in their mind. Therefore, you must be aware of this. The spouse is the one who has been betrayed , and the event that there are things you are to resolve, those problems must be resolved to enable a successful healing process to happen. Make sure that each issue is dealt with properly, as If this doesn't happen then the problems will be resurfacing in your relationship. When the wounds of your emotional life are severe and deep, it would be unreasonable of you to conclude you are recovered and that you do not require to address the issue. Being in a marriage or relationship is a two-person relationship which means that both of you have to collaborate when difficulties occur. Therefore, until you reach a mutual agreement and you discover that your spouse is healing and is in a better place, don't hurry to come to the conclusion that everything is in order.

Stop and stop the matter

One of the best ways to ensure that your spouse builds confidence in you and be healed from the hurt he might be experiencing is to stop and close the relationship immediately. Make sure you inform your spouse the method by which you are planning to end the relationship. Whatever it may be, try to refrain from contact to the other person. If someone else contacts you, make sure you, you inform your partner the fact that it could cause pain to your spouse. Beware of going to locations where you might meet the other person. You can be sure to inform your partner in the event of this happening. Keep reassuring your partner that you do not ever have contact to the person. This will go an important way to restoring the trust that could have been damaged through the scandal and assist your spouse heal quickly.

Talk to your friends about it.

Discussing the situation with your partner could be painful and embarrassing to both. Your spouse might wish to be able to comprehend all the information about the other individual. It is crucial to respond to all questions in a truthful and precise way. If you don't provide details willingly, your spouse might use their imagination to fill in for him or herself the gaps . typically your spouse will come up with the most threatening scenarios. Be aware that your spouse might be required to ask lots of questions frequently. Sometimes , it appears to be the sole thing that your spouse is able to discuss. This is an expected reaction, and you shouldn't be upset or upset over this. There is a possibility that the issue is talked about constantly. As time passes and the healing process begins to have positive effects it will be easier to reduce the amount of discussions. It is important to make sure that the conversation does not take over the marriage or the relationship. In order to ensure that your spouse is repaired and rebuild trust the two of you have to speak and listen to the truth every time. Any attempt to cover up the truth will cause more hurt and create suspicion.

Do not lie.

One of the most costly mistakes you could make is to lie once your spouse discovers that you are involved in an affair. Avoid committing mistruths and lies, secrecy and deceit after you're discovered. Inform your spouse as there is a good chance that they'll continue to ask questions about your relationship to your spouse. Be prepared to answer every question and not be defensive can help your spouse feel more trust and faith in your abilities, making healing more efficient. If you lies, it could cause a lot of problems in building trust and making sure that your spouse recovers quickly. Create a new norm for answering all questions with honesty. This might seem to say but in order to help your spouse recover this is crucially important.

Take responsibility

You have to be accountable to your partner when you are involved in an affair. It is a difficult procedure, but it's essential in helping your partner to be repaired and rebuild trust in your marriage relationship. Your life is now an open book once your spouse finds out that you're involved in an affair. It is necessary for your spouse to view the calls to your cell phone and texts and gain access to all other information that is yours. They may also need to know the location you're going to or where you are working, what you'll be doing, and any alteration to plans. Most of the time it could appear to violate your privacy rights but you'll have to deal the consequences of being involved with someone else in a relationship. Being proactive can help in healing and restore the trust you had before.

Accept and apologize

You need to acknowledge the immense pain that you caused your partner by having an affair. Be sincere in your sorry and show sincerity that you are sincere in this. You'll need to apologize frequently before they are effective and aid in healing. Recognizing the pain and sorrow you've caused your partner It is an essential step towards healing your relationship and rebuilding your relationship. It is important to remember that following the incident, your marriage's history has changed and it's important to acknowledge these changes that have occurred due to the harm that was done in your relationships. It is important to assure your spouse about your positive intentions for your relationship. But, it is important to be aware that apology is essential however it is your actions after the incident which will allow your spouse get back to health quickly.

Make the necessary changes

If you are involved on an affair you have to apologize to your partner in a manner that gives an abundance of significance to them. The amendments you should make are emotional assurance and a demonstration of the trustworthiness of your spouse. Other amends that you make should be more concrete, and can be a symbol of your goodwill and intention toward your spouse. This will demonstrate to your spouse that you're truly committed to ensure that your marriage or relationship is on the right track. If your spouse recognizes this, they is bound to heal very quickly and discover something meaningful in your marriage or relationship.

Learn the causes behind having an affair

People get involved in affairs due to a variety of motives. There are many reasons to be a problem with character, self-absorbed, and an overly narcissistic attitude to life. It is crucial to are aware of the reason to ensure that if the causes appear, you're aware of the negative effects that could result. Some of the reasons that could cause one of the parties in a relationship to engage in an affair are:

* Uncertainty or boredom within the marriage

* Receive more attention from a person

* Feeling lonely or disengaged from your partner or

* Boundary issues

If you were involved in an affair due to any of the reasons listed above It is crucial to discuss the issue with your partner so you can devise ways to address the particular problem. If you can explain to your spouse the reasons you were involved in an affair, they will be able to understand and will assist to ease the hurt the couple may be experiencing. It will also be the first step to build an intimate relationship in the aftermath.

Don't engage in the blame game.

It is important to remember that having an affair isn't the best way to deal with issues that you are experiencing during your marriage. There are plenty of reasons for why you might have been involved in an affair, don't try to blame your spouse, as this can cause the issue to become more difficult to handle. There are many options to consider if your marriage that are experiencing difficulties, for instance, counseling or marriage classes. Talk to your spouse honestly and identify the behavior that you both could need to alter in order to stop this issue from occurring in the future and to have a better union or relationship. Don't be a victim to your spouse because this could result in more pain and make the healing process more difficult.

Do not be impatient

It is important to remember it is possible that recovering trust or healing could be longer than you expected. So, you must remain patient and don't quit during the healing process because it can make things even challenging for the relationships you have. The phases involved in recovery from an affair include:

* Crisis period

* Disorganization

* A loss of faith in the marriage and the partner

* Unshakable dreams

The most effective way to heal is the demonstration of demonstrated behavior and accountability throughout the day. It is important to assure your spouse that you appreciate that they stuck with you and offered an opportunity to give you another shot. You should express your gratitude to your spouse during the healing and rebuilding process.

Do not allow the event be the sole reason for your separation.

Aiding your spouse in healing isn't easy, and it is often overwhelming and difficult. It is therefore important to keep reminding your spouse of the good times and strength you've experienced during your time together. Make sure to recall the beginnings of your relationship. This will trigger positive emotions and convictions towards your partner regardless of what's happened. The confidence that is created is important to make your healing more efficient. This lets you both be re-engaged in your relationship and aid in the process of rebuilding. Make sure your spouse knows that you're trustworthy and it's possible for trust to be restored and to enjoy the same joy you enjoyed prior to the incident.

Accept the anger displayed by your spouse

It can be difficult to believe that your spouse will never let go of their hurt and anger despite the apology that you have made. You've completed all of the inquiries and are willing to go forward with your life. It is possible that you don't be able to comprehend the reason you are pressured to justify every decision you take, so you can explain the direction you're taking, who you will be going with and how long you'll take. A part of helping your spouse heal includes giving them the opportunity to let go of tension and hurt and share this together. Think of this as the beginning of an exciting new level of intimacy and romance. This will enable you to understand how to deal with difficult times. There is no set time that your spouse is willing to let go of the anger. Do not criticize your spouse regardless of whether the anger has made the person accuse you of being abusive. If you take all the things is inside of him or her the person will heal quickly.

Make sure you have expectations

An affair that is not properly handled will certainly cause tension in your marriage or relationship. It is important to be honest about your mistakes and infidelity. Set realistic expectations you are able to achieve. This will let your spouse know that, despite the relationship that you were involved in, you're still dedicated to your spouse and have plans.

Open communication

Be honest to your spouse. Be sure to trust him with your secrets If you want him to be able to trust the same with.

Rejoice with one another completely

Earn respect and show it. Do not argue or insult your partner in front of anyone else.

Love without limits

It is something that you must to be able to do as early as you begin your relationship. It is not possible to love dependent on just what someone else will do for you.

Give yourself time

Spend time with each other. Do things that you both love. Find something common that you both love and there will surely be something that you enjoy.

Join part of a group

Consider yourself part of a team. Be cautious of what you do on behalf of the other. If you are unsure, ask for clarification but don't put forward something that's in a way that is not believable and expect that it will be accepted.

Acceptance

Accept each other and learn to accept mistakes and not be a victim.

Apologize

Accept your apology in a relaxed and easy manner when you commit an error. This means that you must admit to your mistakes. Do not wait for your partner to make an apology.

Forgiveness

Forgive mistakes. Be gracious and gentle when you hear someone apologize, and don't blame your friend for their mistakes.

Cooperate

Partner with your partner in everything he/she needs. Don't assume to be the person who always gets the credit. You must ensure that the needs of your partner are taken care of first.

Pay attention

Always pay attention to your partner while they talk. Be sure to listen completely. Don't listen while looking at the television or with your head in the paper.

Spontaneity

Be spontaneous in your gestures toward your spouse. Make her feel special by giving her a present that she doesn't expect. It could be a gift card you designed or even a gift from the store.

Revitalize your relationship frequently

Set up a date at the end of the day. You can work to keep things interesting and your love will be active for longer.

Beware of dependency too much

Dependence on your partner isn't best for your relationship because you could be getting it destroyed by your partner. This is true for males as well as the females.

Keep yourself healthy

Be sure to take charge of your health and your partner. Unhealthy health can cause you to be cranky, or put the burden of taking care of your healthier partner.

Create an established routine

Establish a routine in which you share activities. Regular, routine activities will bring you closer.

Chapter 13: Healing Your Marriage

Give your spouse the time to grieve.

If your spouse finds out the possibility of another affair, it could cause them to take their breath off. As opposed to trying to alter the emotions of your spouse while the hurt remains fresh you should to give them the time to grieve and reflect. Give them time to grieve as it is one of the best ways to release painful emotions. Be aware that the person is grieving the loss of confidence in your commitment to sexual intimacy. If your partner is talking to you, you could attempt to convince her to go for a walk. This will assist them to digest difficult emotions requires lots of energy, and it's best if your spouse is able to look around and realizes that the world is full of beautiful things to offer despite the destruction the person is suffering.

Talk a lot with your spouse.

If your spouse has to go through this difficult incident, you will need to be able to talk with him or her. You must use effective communication skills to avoid creating more stress for them.

Make sure you talk to each other and that neither one of you becomes overly stressed or defensive. As much as you can to come up with decisions jointly about the type of new life you might want to live after the event. Make sure that the choices you make are mutually beneficial and that they are not a result of any type that compromises you. If you are not able to demonstrate an effective way of communicating You can seek help from a counselor for relationship advice for guidance on how to communicate efficiently.

Establish the foundation to rebuild your relationship.

After an incident, the majority of people will feel it is necessary to talk about the details in a candid manner. In the majority of cases, speaking or hearing about the facts could be extremely painful, similar to as cleaning a painful, dirty wound. You can help your spouse to heal faster by making it simple for them to accept the hurt. Make sure you are honest because telling lies to your spouse could cause a lot of harm in the healing process. When you have a conversation with your spouse, make sure that you're calm and relaxed in order to create an atmosphere more conducive to any constructive conversation that can make your spouse feel relaxed. It is important to work towards getting the other person completely out of the picture. What your spouse is in need of right now is confidence that the person who you had an affair with is now out of the picture completely. Once the truth is revealed it will be simple for your spouse to be free of the pain. Both of you need to understand the reasons behind your decision to get involved in a second affair, as well as the roles that each of you had in the process. This will allow both of you think of strategies to avoid such an incident from happening again in the future. Be sure to avoid a blame games are involved as it will create a painful situation you and your spouse may be facing more challenging. The ability to heal depends on you two and as the perpetrator you have to play a bigger role in restoring the trust that your spouse placed in you.

Build something new and satisfying with your partner.

The simple act of helping your spouse recover from the incident isn't enough. You can create an entirely new, more loving and trusting relationship than you had before. Working together, you can transform your mistakes into great learning opportunities. Create new ways to interact to correct the errors which led to an affair. Develop preventive strategies to ensure that the same event doesn't occur and again so that the wound will be cured permanently.

Discuss the issue with appropriate boundaries

If you're innocent You'll want to question your partner about the specifics of the incident. Some innocent partners will run as the cheating partner in every detail, while others will only be able to deal with the essential details. The partner who is cheating must be aware of the emotions of the innocent partner and only reveal the information requested. Discussion of specifics of the incident is a sensitive topic and should be handled with care and the appropriate boundaries. Make sure the time for discussion is not interrupted by distractions. Allow enough time to discuss the subject, but make it brief enough to avoid an argument that is heated. The two partners should alternate talking uninterrupted. Be careful not to criticize and judgemental with one another in this highly emotional conversation. The goal is to establish a clear line of communication, letting the cheater share enough information to answer the most basic questions you ask yourself. A crucial thing to keep in mind is not to ask your partner with details regarding his love interest. The information you gather will only result in more emotional pain and anger for both of you. It was among the most difficult experiences for me as I was eager to learn every detail about my husband's partner. However, doing this only made me unhappy and angry. Instead, focus on building your relationship, as this will help you get closer as two people.

Find the causes

To build an effective relationship, first discover what issues within the marriage led to it. Every one of you has brought memories of childhood trauma and experiences of infidelity that affect the way you communicate with your spouse. Consider the traumas that occurred during your childhood and discuss how they have affected your trust and the way you conduct yourself in your current actions. Although you might not be able to figure out every negative factor which contributed to your unhygienic behaviors and convictions but you and your spouse should meet and try to address the main issues. This will allow you to understand the perspectives of each other and what they expect. It is also a good idea to talk about any major recent incidents in your life that could contribute to the difficulties at home.

Change how you think and how you feel

Once you've identified the most important problems, you can develop an action plan to create a more intimate relationship. Before you can begin it is essential to establish the right mindset and emotions. Many couples who are affected by infidelity have an attitude of negativity. They believe that the future of their relationship is uncertain or that they believe that their partner is not capable of changing. Should you and your spouse get caught up in this type of negative thoughts, you'll have an extremely difficult time recovering.

Your partner and you should be optimistic about the future. A lot of couples who are sincerely working on reestablishing their marriage have greater intimacy. Eliminate any doubts about your partner that you cannot change, and let him know that you are confident that he will make your relationship stronger. Work through your issues one by one. When you have success early on, the two of you remain going in the direction of change.

Avoid emotional outbursts with negative connotations.

An affair may trigger feelings of hurt, anger and frustration. It is easy for two people to treat one another with disrespect and shouting. These kinds of behaviors could quickly ruin a safe atmosphere to heal. Be sure to treat one another with respect, speaking in a non-judgmental, caring manner and avoiding excessive demands from one another. Be careful not to punish your partner by taking an exercise. This can only squelch feelings of affection from your partner, and can trigger anger.

Make sure you reach a consensus in addressing questions

Your partner and you will each have different views in making the decision together. This is that each person's attitude and opinions are shaped by their particular experiences and the family environment. It is easy to become involved in an argument that is heated in a relationship where each person believes that things should be handled their way. If you are able to talk about matters with a non-judgmental mindset and an open-minded mind, you'll be able to come to an outcome that is win-win. Additionally, you'll develop a greater sense of intimacy by showing your partner you appreciate their views and emotions. In discussions, you should be sure to discuss the other's views with respect, and try not to tear down any ideas. It is important to briefly summarize your partner's point perspective so that he will know that you've been paying attention. Then, think of ways to solve the problem. After you've completed the above steps, then you'll choose the best solution for the issue.

Establishing an emotional connection

This is among the most crucial steps in your recovery from marital problems. Many problems arise because marriage relationships was not able to meet the partner's emotional requirements. When a couple discovers that a different person is able to provide the things lacking in their relationship, he'll become addicted to the new partner. If, however, you're among those who are afflicted by someone who is an insidious cheater, it is recommended to consult a professional for help to determine whether your relationship is worthy of saving. There's no perfect union that exists. Every relationship struggles when it comes to establishing more emotional intimacy. There are times when couples fall into the same one-two step routine and dance routine, but they never seem to be in sync with respect to satisfying their partner's emotional needs. Every couple has a distinct style of love that has been learned from them in the early years of the early years of their lives. If you have a bad experience in your childhood and it impacts the way you love in subsequent relationships. This is called attachment theory. When couples with different romantic styles seek to be emotionally connected the argument can begin. Couples who experienced emotional support and emotional comfort from their parents in the time of trauma may not receive the same the comfort of the self-sufficient partner due to the fact that their parents did not provide emotional comfort. Only when you understand the love styles of your partner can you begin to understand how to connect with them emotionally at the deepest level. If your partner was raised without emotional support from their parents and a teacher, they learned to keep emotions in and became independent and care for their own needs.

Create positive memories

Begin to create lasting memories of your relationship with them. At present, you may have a negative view of your partner and don't have the motive to treat your partner with love and respect. But, to improve your relationship with your partner, you must not wait for your thoughts to change. Research has shown that engaging in positive behavior and doing good things for your partner will in turn alter the way you think and act toward your partner. Be a good person and show love to your partner! Thinking about positive times within your relationship can to rekindle the love and feelings you have for your partner. Make time to look through old photo albums and journals. Reading old love letters written during your courtship days can bring back good memories. Another tip is to talk about your various experiences and how it was growing up with your family. This will help your spouse recognize your distinctive ways of being and behavior.

Make a plan for weekly fun time.

It's easy to get caught up in the day-to-day routine tasks of work chores, household chores, and caring for the children. As a mother of two kids I understand how difficult it is to spend time with your spouse. If both you and your spouse are busy and have no time for one another I encourage you to take a step back from your hectic lifestyle. The relationship you share will never develop in intimacy if you don't spend sufficient time together. It's easy to slip into the same routine of life. An active lifestyle can pull you and your spouse apart, just as it did with my marriage. Soon, your relationship will turn into only a matter of roommates. This is the perfect scenario that allows for an illicit affair to take place. To avoid this it is important to schedule regular dates with your partner in order to keep the romance burning. This can be challenging to manage in the beginning because you and your partner might be uncomfortable spending time together with nothing to talk about. However, I guarantee you that when you do the routine of planning and carrying out Do things with your partner the feelings of love will return. Are you able to recall the excitement and excitement that you shared as you and your significant other first began dating? The reality is that most relationships cannot last forever. Additionally, everyday routines and responsibilities can take away the important feeling of intimacy and closeness. Research has shown that the absence of a love relationship could fool your brain into reviving feelings of passion and excitement simply by doing exciting and new things. It is a good idea to visit a new place together , or even try diving together. The exciting new experiences can stimulate your brain to feel the same excitement and passion you felt when you first began dating.

Be a great listener

Communication is essential to reestablishing relationships. However, you won't be able to effectively communicate if you don't develop the skills to be a great listener. We often think we know what our counterpart is saying. We all do it. that I'm guilty of this. There were numerous times that I assumed that my friend intended and then reacted inappropriately, which resulted in an argument. Sometimes, you only hear what you wish to believe or believe. Do not make this error. Instead, you should refrain from speaking the same way that you've always done, and concentrate on the aim of building a connection through positive interactions. Get rid of sarcastic comments in exchange for comments which express how you feel. If your partner is talking pay attention to the motives behind the words they are talking about. Be sure not to disrupt your companion. It's crucial to show respect for your partner and to respect the words he or she's saying. If your partner has done speaking, try to repeat what he or she was saying and try to comprehend the emotions behind the words.

Recommit yourself regularly to the connection

The process of recovering your relationship from infidelity is a lengthy journey. It's not easy to let go of the hurt and hurt caused from the affair. There is also the possibility of carrying anger towards your partner for sabotaging your trust. The process of letting the anger go takes time. The pain and memory of the incident will never go away however, its effects will fade with time.

If you're looking to get your relationship back on the right path I suggest you concentrate on forgiveness for your partner so your healing can start. I suggest this when your partner is truly sorry for what happened and is sincerely committed to making the relationship work. When you and your spouse are working to build relationships that are emotionally intimate and replace negative behaviors and communications by more positive behaviors it is inevitable that you will be disappointed and suffer setbacks in the process. To reduce the frequency of disappointments, you need to set realistic goals and expectations for healing.

Chapter 14: Ideas To Rebuild Sexual Safety

This list provides a structure for dialog. Sexual repair requires:

* The willingness of both parties to do what is necessary to make the recovery.

Conversations with adults that emphasize the concepts of vulnerability, safety and confidence.

* Acceptance and understanding of the spouse who was affected by the betrayal of sexual affection.

* Courtship concepts that focus on the emotional bond in which the parties can talk eye-to-eye and talk to one another while offering safe, non-sexual physical contact (e.g. holding hands or cuddling) with no sexual expectation.

* Establishing sexual safety. Many therapists and 12-step programs advocate a 90-day cooling-off duration (abstinence) to strengthen the relationship as well as help the victim abstain from sexual activity in order to see the bigger picture of his behavior issues. Concerns about sexually protected sex and sexual sobriety should

be addressed. Infractions that undermine sexual fidelity are dealt with by an "no" (purposeful safeguarding) and boundaries that are aimed at fixing trust.

Discussion about the best way to reengage sexually. Abstinence is often utilized as a way to get through the beginning stages of trauma from betrayal to protect the partner. In marriages where sobriety is still the main goal, a fresh process of establishing a healthy sexual and emotional connections can be initiated. Abstinence isn't meant to be a permanent where you can stay.

Then, you can decide what and when partners want to reconnect in sexual intimacy. Are you more at ease with the lights off or on? Do you feel more comfortable in your clothing switched off or on? It is possible to ask your spouse to walk through this by asking what you need to do to get them to engage.

Chapter 15: Common Errors To Avoid

When you are helping your spouse get over an incident, there are frequent mistakes to be aware of to ensure success. Here are 9 most common mistakes to avoid.

• Lying about certain aspects of the incident. There is no need to ever attempt to cover up the incident that you participated in. If you want your spouse to heal effectively, or rebuild trust with your spouse, you have to speak the truth and nothing except the truth. The efforts to heal and reconcile must be based on honesty and not less. If your spouse is aware that you're not honest when you provide details, he or she might develop a negative view which can cause the healing process to become even more complicated.

* Try to repair the injury as fast as possible. Don't do the wrong thing by telling your spouse to ignore the issue or to avoid discussing the matter. It is important to realize how your partner is grieving and bleeding. Keep your eyes open even when it takes a long period of time for healing to

be completed. Be aware that people have different times to heal. The speed of healing may also not last so allow healing to be able to take its course.

• Lack of empathy. Do not think of not be aware of the harm that you've caused your spouse and to your relationship as a whole when you had an affair.

* Game of blame. Be careful not to shift blame to different forces or situations outside of your control. Accept full responsibility for your actions and statements. It can be a disaster if try to blame the problem on your spouse in this period when he/she suffers. It could cause another injury that will not be able to heal in the future or cause your marriage or your relationship end up breaking. This will let your spouse know that you've accepted the burden and assist in the healing process.

* Being violent. It is not advisable to be aggressive or violent. You will probably be upset, but do not use your anger to commit violence, as this could cause the wound to become more severe. Be

ready to listen to the truth, and to hear things that you might not wish to be able to hear. If you are feeling that you'd like to put off the issue for the next day to integrate the information you just received You are able to do that.

• Not being patient with your spouse's communications. If you want your spouse to be healed it is essential to be patient. It is crucial to allow your spouse to speak out all the issues so that the pain will come out of them. Let your spouse let go of all anger and other emotions that they are carrying within them. For example, if your spouse is crying , let your spouse to cry as hard as they want to. Crying is one method to ease pain completely.

* Leave the entire process to God. It is quite common for people to put everything to God's care when faced with difficulties. However, this doesn't be the case all the time. The best way to proceed is request God to examine your soul and discover whether there's anything that you have yet to address. Examine if there's something left to be dealt with that might hinder healing. Then, you can request God to restore your heart and

your emotions. Request him to control your thoughts and break. He can also help you end the relationship with your partner. God is a wonderful healer, but all things must not be left to him.

* Pride. Avoid pride at all costs as it can cause the hurt you that you caused your spouse to be more severe. After an affair, be humble and admit your error. Making a show of encouraging can hurt your partner more, as they could think it is a sign of arrogance. Do not worry about the fact that you did something wrong. Make apologia to your spouse rather than trying to prove that you are also acknowledged or prove that you are able to have done the things you did.

Chapter 16: Resolving The Scores And Giving Up Infidelity

Discovering that your spouse or husband is not faithful could be shocking and adjusting with the reality is just as difficult of a task. You're suddenly confronted by the fact that your trust in the relationship is broken and you're not sure whether you've got it in you to believe that you can still have hope.

There is no one who enters an engagement hoping to be divorced by a partner. Many couples enter into the marriage contract hoping for the most ideal outcome. However, the reality is that it doesn't result as you'd like itto, regardless of whether you're up to accept it or not. There will be instances when you be dissatisfied. After overcoming the initial shock, and then finding out that infidelity is making it's ways into the relationship of your partner, what's next? How do you deal with the unpleasant truth without losing your sense of sanity or self-confidence?

Although your initial reaction may be to defend your defenses and defend yourself The best thing you can do is to not do anything whatsoever. It might take all the self-control and courage you have and it's certainly better than doing something that you'll regret later on in the future. Knee-jerk reactions are often typically characterized by despair, and if you don't want to make any foolish decisions, it's better to be calm and let the emotional rollercoaster. When you decide to stay still you're deciding to remain in a steady place and let your rationality be in charge.

What happens when infidelity enters into a Marriage?

The majority of marriages start with complete trust, but in the course of time, things can sever that trust. It doesn't matter if it's a nagging suspicion that your spouse is having an affair with an individual on the other side, or the late night texts and phone calls that make you stay up all the wee hours of the night, it's difficult to shake off that anxiety, particularly when the evidence starts piling up.

If you are looking to begin with the process of rebuilding it is essential to be aware of the negative effects of breaking trust in a relationship. It is important to comprehend how deeply the damage is before you can begin any kind of damage control. The truth is challenging and painful, but it's the only way you can recuperate and heal from the injury.

More Risky Insecurities

The first thing to happens to an individual after trust is a sudden decrease in self-esteem. When someone feels betrayed their self-esteem gets affected as it causes them to doubt their own worthiness. Anyone who discovers that their spouse or husband has been cheating is likely to start accepting their fears. If insecurity takes over and you begin to feel anxious, it's likely that the marriage and trust to fall apart from there.

Continuous anxiety

Another result of infidelity is continuous anxiety. If a person begins giving to the fear of being insecure the natural reaction is to worry about the stability of their relationship. When the foundations have been being shaken, they are concerned over the prospects for their relationship. This constant worry can cause anxiety and anger that can result in the breaking and dissolution of their relationship. The anxiety should not be taken lightly as, once it takes over, it could be difficult to overcome or overcome.

Unstable moods

A lack of trust or stability can cause either spouse giving in to anger or depression. Infidelity can cause feelings to flare You'll never know the kind of mood one of the spouses will be in on any given day. From anger to sadness or resentment Couples who have to deal with infidelity are vulnerable to mood swings, particularly the spouse who is grieving.

Loss of intimacy

If you mix the negative self-esteem, unjustified anxiety and depression The relationship will then lose its intimacy. If one person is insecure about their partner, that causes the other partner to pull away due to anger or guilt. Intimacy decreases when either or both parties are more focused on pain and hurt, and not on the resolution of conflicts. The worst part is, once the intimacy is gone, there's no reason to fight over the relationship. If there isn't cooperation between both spouses, losing intimacy is the final straw for divorce or separation.

Do you feel like it's all familiar to you? If you've been struggling in the aftermath for more than you've ever thought now is the time to take your first step to move forward. It may be an easy option at the moment however the longer you allow the hurt take over you, the more difficult it will be to overcome it. It is essential to dig deeper and learn to trust yourself once more.

The first person to become confident with is you. It's crucial to start trusting in yourself if you wish to take control of the circumstances. If you allow the situation to dictate your actions, you'll find yourself feeling a bit lost and insecure. No matter what you've been through in the past; nobody is entitled to ever feel helpless when faced with a situation.

It's important to do not get caught up in your own blame games. In spite of who is at fault You shouldn't get caught in the trap of accusing yourself or your spouse for the issue. Instead, you should focus on actions that help you to become stronger and work towards healing. Don't let infidelity destroy the person you are or break your relationship because, ultimately, you're the one who calls the shots.

Trust may be damaged however this doesn't mean you should abandon your marriage and cause the end of your relationship. It is possible to use this chance to create something new but also to strengthen the relationship between you and your partner. However, before you can repair any issue with your spouse or husband be sure to make time to work through your own problems first. The following chapters will instruct you how to handle the aftermath, regardless of whether you're the cheater or was the victim of cheating.

For the One Who Betrayed

If you are the spouse who has cheated in the past, you are a source of responsibility to repair your marriage that is broken. Accepting the consequences is only part of the process. It is also important to get rid of guilt.

If your partner was the one who was the one to commit infidelity, you must be aware the possibility of reconciliation so long as you're prepared to do the work. It takes patience, honesty and a sense of humility on your behalf to put the pieces that were broken back together. The good news isthat you'll be able to restore the trust you lost in the event that your spouse appreciates your sincerity throughout this entire process. Here are some tips to remember.

Never compromise on Honesty Once

Whatever was it that caused the infidelity, be it the result of a miscommunication or just a one-night affair or personal struggles It's time to admit it. It's not possible to begin the next stage of your recovery without telling your spouse the truth. In addition to being honest with yourself and your partner, you must be able to accept what you are truly thinking about. Honesty can take away your self-esteem however, over the long run it will assist you to build a stronger connection with your loved one, and gain a fresh perspective. If you begin to be truthful, you'll set yourself free from the shackles of lies, and there'll no longer be a reason to keep a secret any longer.

Stop playing the Blame Game or playing your old Mind Games

Blaming the spouse who is grieving is silly, as is engaging in mind-games. It doesn't matter if believe that your motives are valid however, it doesn't give the right to place the burden on your partner. Remember that the choice was yours to make. Nobody made you cheat on your spouse or your husband. You're still accountable for your choices. The most you can do is to show regret and show compassion towards your spouse. It is important to demonstrate that you're willing to rectify your mistakes. If you are seeking to defend your errors you're probably in need of talk about your concerns with a professional.

Do Not Keep Anything From Your Partner Ever Again

Your spouse has every right to be aware of the truth, when you reach the point at which he/she starts asking questions, be sure you respond to all of them. Even if it is hurtful, it's more beneficial to admit the truth instead of spending for the rest of your life by hiding behind lies. Let your grieving spouse be the first to confront you. So, you don't feel like you're being scolded when the spouse responds with delicate questions. The most important thing to heal is open communication, so even if you hurt, it's at this point that you have to begin being sincere again.

You can give your spouse what he or She Likes

If your spouse is making demands on you do not just put the person down. Check to see if the demands made by your spouse are acceptable enough to adhere to. If your spouse advises you to stay clear of the person you had a relationship with By all means it is best to stay away. You're not in a position to compromise or ask the things he or she would like. In order to reestablish your relationship, you have to prove yourself. So make sure you do the best way to earn confidence back. Be open to what the other person says and try to avoid dismissing any ideas right from the beginning. Discuss the actions you could take to gain their confidence back. If you're willing to take on the effort, it doesn't mean you're not a good person to be. Be sure to meet their wants and needs, but not to the extent that you're sacrificed for yourself.

Let the Time heal the Wounds

It's possible that you're not at a great place with your spouse today however, over time, you'll realize that time can heal any hurts. Keep in mind that you're not the one who must process the events that occurred. Your spouse also requires space and time to sort out their own problems, therefore, be considerate of the time to breathe. Always take the opportunity to inform your spouse that you're here for the long run. Make sure your spouse or husband know that you'll keep waiting until they are willing to speak to you and build your relationship. While you wait you can take a break to do some thinking about yourself.

for the one who was Conceived On

If you're the spouse who was cheating on and you're carrying many hurts and regret within your heart. At this point, it might seem as if you don't are able to be able to accept forgiveness, however remember that you're getting to forgiveness. Forgiveness is only one part of the battle since in the end, you have to be in a position to let go of the situation and start from with a fresh start.

For the spouse who was hurt by infidelity, be strong and be aware it's possible to reconcile so long as you're willing to open you heart and mind to the person who hurts once more. It's true that this won't occur over night, but you do need to be ready to make that first step. The good thing is that making the move is actually more simple than you imagine. It's just a matter of taking the day by day approach and remain positive.

Be sure to know your facts

Don't let your emotions take the best of you. If you are letting your thoughts or you let your thoughts wander ensure that you've got your facts in order. Do not confront your spouse using just gossip as your primary evidence. It is essential to be 100 100% certain there is no cheating between your partner and your before you begin a fight. When you have evidence that you believe is true, then present your spouse with calm and in a rational manner. Whatever the circumstance your spouse still has the right to be treated as an individual human being.

Write down your thoughts in writing

The process of expressing your emotions can be overwhelming, but expressing them through writing can assist you in coming to terms with your pain and pain. Even whether you're not a skilled author, it's possible to discover much about the issue and yourself by putting your emotions into words. If you're feeling nervous about writing everything down, you can start by using an uncluttered notebook and make notes. It's also a great method to track your progression.

Find someone you can count on

It's also beneficial to have someone to chat with. It doesn't matter if it's a counselor an expert in life coaching, or a pastor, it's crucial to find someone you can discuss your feelings with. A professional can provide you with an insight into the situation can help you deal with it better and move forward quicker. Make sure you choose an expert who will offer an impartial opinion, particularly when you're still trying to figure out the issues you have between your partner. It isn't a good idea to have someone who will take sides.

Pause and take a deep breath

After all the nights of sleepless nights and heartaches, it's time to have a break. Do not be afraid to take some time to relax and distance yourself from the battle. If you're in need of some time to yourself and be quiet to think about what's happening Don't be afraid of getting away from the battle for a few minutes. In the end, you're entitled to time to reflect on your thoughts.

Send a letter to your spouse

This isn't a must however, if you think that you must be willing to do it, then compose a letter to your spouse. A letter can allow you to express the emotions you feel in a manner that doesn't appear as an attack on your spouse. Inform your loved ones what you truly are feeling in the most transparent way you can. Do not write anything you'll regret later and be careful with exclamations. Although there's no exact method to write this crucial letter, the most effective approach to overcome this is to draft some drafts prior to when you compose your final one. In this way, you will not have to write your spouse a nasty letter.

4 The Signs That a Marriage Is worth saving

Let's face it for a few minutes. Even if you've taken the first steps toward reconciliation, there's no assurance that your spouse will not harm you in the future. In the present, there's no way to tell whether you'll have an everlasting blissful relationship, or if all the efforts are wasted. The only thing you are certain of has been that the circumstances are changing and resolving this situation is going to require hard work for each of you.

If you're thinking of trying again with your marriage however, you're not certain if you're making correct choice There are four indicators to be on the lookout for. If you notice a mix of these indicators, it suggests that your relationship could be worth keeping.

Better Communication Lines

Communication is essential to a successful relationship. It plays a important role when you're in the process of reestablishing your marriage after an affair. It's hard to restore relationships after suffering an affair however if this experience can help you improve your relationships with one another and you're able to communicate better, there could be a chance to salvage your relationship. If you're not ready to improve communicating aspects of your relationship, it's time to put it down.

Transparency is encouraged

Transparency isn't necessarily the first thing that pops into the mind following an infidelity incident However, if both parties decide to repair their relationship, it is feasible. Transparency happens when both spouses commit to never keep secrets from one another. It is a promise to discuss all aspects of your lives with your spouse and never keep anything secret from one another and again. Being transparent is a great indication that you're taking the initiative and doing your part to restore trust to the relationship. Don't pressure your spouse to reveal information if they're not prepared for this yet. Set the example and create an environment of trust and confidence which will inspire your spouse to be more honest.

It's an Team Effort

The marriage operates in a way that resembles one, and you should not ever feel like you're the sole person working. It is important to believe that you're all in it together for the long haul in order to achieve success. If you feel as if you're on opposite sides and you're left with no option other than to defend your spouse. It becomes more difficult when each small argument becomes an argument over control. When you feel as though you're on one team with your spouse, you begin to look at the bigger picture and appreciate your spouse's work. It isn't important which side is right or wrong so long as you are focused to the same end.

The Relationship has Improved

It's hard to believe that something good can be derived from infidelity, but if you keep a clear mind it could help improve your marriage. Because in every storm, you can decide to look for the bright side. If your experience with infidelity has made the marriage more stable, it's certainly worth resolving to work on. Take a look at where your relationship stands from a perspective of the 'now' and determine whether you are able to be sure that your spouse is trustworthy again. If you focus on the present it will be easier to observe and appreciate the growth in your relationship which will aid you in making the right choice.

Conclusion

Congrats on reaching the conclusion in the story!

In reality, the person you've been the most trusting in this life as well as the one you love dearly or the one you believe to be your spouse has been cheating on you will cause you to suffer that it will suffocate your soul and cause you to feel like all the world has abandoned you. It is difficult to know what you should do and you're devastated. You aren't sure whether you should offer your partner another chance to prove that he regrets the actions he took.

However, you must be strong, brave , and accepting. If they decide they'd like to stay with you and prove to you they're worthy of this in all it's worth, allow them another chance at it , because everyone deserves another chance. If, after this chance they get into another relationship or stop altogether, it is time to end the affair. Inform them that they're unworthy of your attention, and advise them that you're better than them.

Do not let this incident alter your opinion of yourself as you are stunning, beautiful and amazing and you'll outlast this. Whatever you decide to do is the best thing to do stick to your decision fight for it, and you'll be able to see that marriages don't always work but when two couples will be willing to put in the effort that, absolutely it's worth the struggles.

www.ingramcontent.com/pod-product-compliance
Lightning Source LLC
Chambersburg PA
CBHW050404120526
44590CB00015B/1821